DEDICATION

This book is dedicated to two women in my career who had a profound impact on my life. First is Barbara MacDonald, an incredible food-service professional, who was my mentor from the age of 16 years to 32 years. Sadly, she passed away when I was 32. She helped me both personally and professionally. In large part, my career in the hospitality industry was shaped by her knowledge, shared values, cooking, and love of learning. She was authentic, visionary, and a heart-centered leader.

The second person I want to acknowledge is Eileen Crowley Reed. She was a high-performance consultant and former attorney, before enjoying her retirement. She became my mentor when I was in higher education. When I think back to that first impression she made on me, I thought I wanted to be just like her. She had a grace and authenticity about her. She was well-educated, experienced, eclectic, and had depth. I admired the way she could communicate at all levels of the organization — from senior management or hourly employees — in her role as a consultant. She invested her time and talent in me. I believe much of my success is because of Eileen's influence in my life and for that, I will be forever grateful.

Kim Nugent

WHAT READERS ARE SAYING ABOUT PROMOTION PROTOCOL™

Dr. Kim Nugent has spent her entire career developing leaders at all levels. She is an authority on performance, talent. and leadership. In this book, Dr. Nugent provides a fresh perspective on leadership development along with a new coaching framework. Emerging leaders and experienced leaders alike will find new insights worth reading in Promotion Protocol!

— **Eddie Turner, The Leadership Excelerator™, Executive & Leadership Coach, Facilitator, Keynote Speaker and National Media Commentator**

Many people speak about leadership these days and Dr. Kim Nugent is the ideal mentor for exceptional leadership because she is personally a proven, effective, and exceptional leader. Her deep and comprehensive mastery of communication strategies and empowering language has allowed her to create a ground-breaking new approach to transformational dialogue. It's my belief that Dr. Nugent's methodology will become a foundational practice in every organization desiring to cultivate inspirational leaders within their corporate culture. The world needs more exceptional leaders and Dr. Kim Nugent has developed the tools and the guidance in her books and programs to motivate and mentor the next generation of leaders who will bring us forward in bold and exciting ways.

— **Kristen White,
Author of #1 Bestseller, Voice: How to Share your Message, Products and Business with the World.**

Dr. Nugent has made it her career goal to develop individuals within her organization and coaching and encouraging them along the way in a manner that brings out the best in each employee. Her top priority has always been preparing them for their future and she has a long list of successes. This book is an extension of her career accomplishments and is a must-read for your personal career success.

— **Roger Walter, SPHR, Senior Professional in Human Resources**

Kim Nugent nails it! Kim Nugent understands what communication means and how to cut through the difficulties of motivating staff to achieve maximum performance. Her technique educates employees as to their responsibilities to the organization as well as to themselves and their future.

— **Douglas Horn, Past Senior VP. for Patriot American/ Wyndham International**

This book does an exceptional job at providing you with practical, balanced, and engaging tools to change the landscape from employee and employer to mentee and mentor. Regardless of whether you are at the top already trying to help others get there or climbing your way there, this book provides you with a clear, guided path.

— **Cassandra Gaudet, Owner, Real Living by Cass**

Commerce has become very fast-paced and often the most critical conversations with rising talent that will lead to increased revenue are cut short, as time is at a premium. Promotion Protocol is right on-time for where business is today. It allows for employees to have a clear lens on expectations to be promoted through a well-outlined process. This is a great tool for the seasoned manager looking for new ways to work with talent and for a new leader who is just beginning the leadership journey. The clear framework for both the employee and employer on what the organization needs to succeed is genius.

— **Susanne Behrens, College President**

This book really couldn't have come at a better time in my life and my career. I have worked at my company now for 11 years, I am currently a mid-level manager and have been in my current role for 4 years. As I anticipate the next step and what I need to make myself better, this book provided a lot of clarity and questions that I needed to ask myself. Over the next 26 weeks I am going to practice all 26 chapters with each of my employees. I am anxious to see their results as well as my own. I will report back in 26 weeks with the results!

— **Frank Childs, National Oilwell Vargo**

Promotion Protocol™
Unlock the Secrets of Promotability & Career Success
Copyright © 2018 by Dr. Kim Nugent. All rights reserved

ALL RIGHTS RESERVED. This book contains material protected under International and Federal Copyright Laws and Treaties. Any unauthorized reprint or use of this material is prohibited. No part of this book may be reproduced or transmitted in any form or by any means, electronic or mechanical, including photocopying, recording, or by any information storage and retrieval system without express written permission from the author/publisher.

Publisher: Sojourn Publishing
Paperback ISBN: 978-1-62747-272-2
EBook ISBN. 978-1-62747-276-0

Contact Dr. Kim Nugent at:
Email: Kim@PromotionProtocol.com
Web: PromotionProtocol.com | DrNugentSpeaks.com

Credits:
Cover Designers: Gagan Sarkaria, M.F.A, M.B.A, & Abbey Wilkerson, B.F.A. UnfoldYourSuccess.com
Interior Layout & Design: Gagan Sarkaria & Abbey Wilkerson
Book Cover Sales Copy & Content Editing: Gagan Sarkaria
Author Photo: Lisa Crosby

Promotion Protocol Complete Branding, Art Direction, Design & Production: Gagan Sarkaria & Abbey Wilkerson
Presentation / Slide Deck Designer: Gagan Sarkaria
eBooks: Gagan Sarkaria & Abbey Wilkerson

PROMOTION PROTOCOL™

Unlock the Secrets of
Promotability & Career Success

Kim Nugent, Ed.D.

Kim Nugent

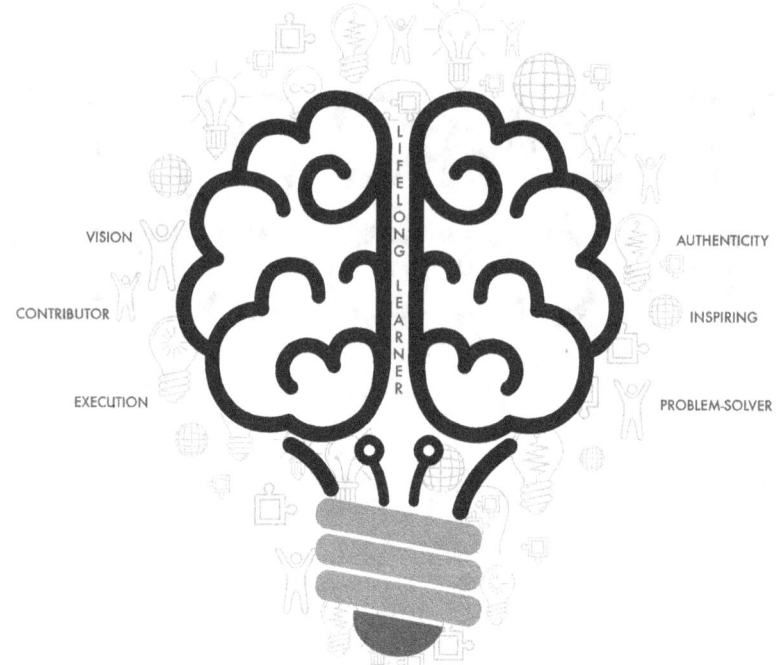

PROMOTION PROTOCOL™

www.PromotionProtocol.com

PROMOTION PROTOCOL

Unlock the Secrets of Promotability and Career Success Purpose

This book is a practical and time-saving guide to help a new generation become promotable while allowing the coach to set expectations in a way that supports the organizational culture and the coach and employee relationship. Specifically, it allows the coach/supervisor and mentee an opportunity to come together each week to discuss a specific trait and allows time for self-assessment and reflection. The purpose of the coaching questions for each trait is for the coach and mentee to learn from each other. Through this collaboration, young talent will be nurtured to step into their future, and in the process, senior leaders can leave their legacy.

The purpose of this book is to provide a coaching framework that allows the supervisor and employee to collaborate on the promotion pathway. It capitalizes on the experience of the supervisor and includes the uniqueness of a new generation of employees. This book has multiple applications and audiences. It can be used for employees wanting to be promoted. The book can be used for middle-level managers to develop their own skills and pro-motability of their employees that are accountable to them. It can be used by senior leaders to transform their coaching ability and build a culture while leaving a legacy. This book can be used as a guide for a college internship class. This book can used by Career Services Directors to assist college students to become more self-aware before entering the workforce and get started on the right path. The book can be used with staff recruiters to assist getting people back to work.

The most effective workplace model in business is coaching; not training.

It is my desire that all employees have special role models who serve as mentors in your life that can help guide and coach you along your promotion and leadership journey. We all need coaches and mentors who can help guide both soft and hard skills. Think about someone you admire or want to emulate as your mentor. Ask them if they would be willing to coach you. You must also be prepared with your own set of questions. It is a dialogue. Coaches and mentors change over time as you change, and that is okay. This might be a new concept for you to have a business coach or professional mentor. Think of it this way. If you like to work out and want to maximize your training efforts, you hire a personal trainer. If you want to lose weight, you might hire a nutritionist or join a weight-loss program. You do this to have someone help you reach your goal and build accountability. Given the fact that this is your career, why not consider hiring a professional coach to jump start your career pathway? If you don't have one, get one. Choose wisely.

Promotion Protocol

TABLE OF CONTENTS

SECTION 1:

Dedication..
Testimonials...
Purpose ....

SECTION 2:

My Story 1
The Reality of the Workplace Today 21
Ever Wonder Why You are Not Getting Promoted? 25
What is your Motivation for a Promotion? 31
Characteristics of High Potential Candidates 35
Keys to Being Promoted – Survey Said 39
The Solution 43
Getting to Know You Guide 47
Self-Assessment Inventory Instructions 51
A Self-Assessment Inventory 52

SECTION 3:

The Solution For Leaders And The New Generation
Of Aspiring Leaders..57
A is for Attitude 60
B is for Brand 70
C is for Communication 80
D is for Depth 88

E is for Energy 94

F is for Focus 102

G is for Gratitude 110

H is for Habits 118

I is for Integrity 128

J is for Jaded 138

K is for Knowledgeable 144

L is for Life-long Learner 154

M is for Mindset 164

N is for Network 174

O is for Opportunity 182

P is for Problem Solver 188

Q is for Question 194

R is for Responsibility 202

S is for Self-Awareness 210

T is for Thank You 218

U is for Unique 226

V is for Vision 232

W is for White Lies 238

X is for X-Factor 244

Y is for Yearning 252

Z is for Zone 260

SECTION 4:

Summary 273

References 279

MY STORY

I have had the privilege of rising to the top of my career in three separate industries. First, in the hospitality industry, serving as General Manager for several hotel chains and Divisional Manager for Hilton Hotels, Inc. Second, in higher education as a University President for several institutions and VP of Faculty Development for a major education corporation. Third, as a best-selling author. I can assure you it was not easy, and I made plenty of mistakes along the way. What I can say is that I am resilient and learn from my mistakes, so I do not repeat them. I do not dwell on adverse situations, as I have seen people do. This stops them and keeps them stuck. Instead, my approach is to get into action to produce the result.

I think I fell in love with being a leader and assuming leadership roles from an early age. I am the oldest of six children. As you can imagine, much responsibility fell on me in the family. My parents had high expectations, provided a great deal of feedback and made me accountable for my sisters and brothers. Truthfully, at the time, I am not sure I appreciated these life lessons as much as I do now. We were raised in a very strict, German, Catholic family. My parents taught all of us the value of a strong work ethic, integrity, responsibility, to be open-minded, embrace diversity, and not to be afraid to try new things.

At age 14, the last thing I wanted to do was to take on babysitting jobs. I already had done that for my family. Debbie, a friend of mine in the neighborhood, told me about a job opening at Hannah's Pies where she worked. I applied and got the job. Obtaining a job referral from my friend Debbie was the beginning of my first experience of understanding the power of your network. I had no idea what that meant at the time.

I went to work for a local pie shop as a waitress and baker. It was super exciting to have a job at that age, to get a paycheck, and learn about people and life. Within eight months, I was promoted to the position of Assistant Manager. How cool is that? It was because I worked hard, was a quick learner and showed up for each shift on time in the proper uniform. I found my passion for the hospitality industry and feel so blessed it happened at such an early age.

When I was a junior in high school, I was in DECA (Distributive Education Clubs of America), where you take high-school classes for half a day and work the other half. Today this is now referred to as career and technology educational programs. I knew I did not want to work in retail, so I asked my teacher, Jean Samples, if I could work for a restaurant. It took some convincing because students had only worked in retail and no DECA student had worked in the restaurant industry to date, but my teacher was open to the idea. At the same time, I was to compete at a regional conference in job interviewing. My teacher needed me to get some real practice, so she sent me to a Human Resources Director of a major retail corporation. The HR Director did not know anything about food service and wanted the practice session to be as real as possible, so she set up an interview for me with the store's restaurant manager, Barbara McDonald. It was great practice for me. Two things happened as a result; I won the regional DECA job-interviewing competition, and Barbara, the restaurant manager, was so impressed with me that she offered me a job as her assistant. It was not easy. Most of the staff were much older than I and were from different ethnic backgrounds. The kitchen employees did not like me and made that quite clear. It was part of their informal, kitchen-line indoctrination process to see if I was strong enough to deal with the stress. Each day after I finished my shift, I would go to the locker room and cry. Over time, I won each of them over with my hard work, determination, and the desire to learn from them. I might have wanted to quit, but I did not want to disappoint Barbara, as she took a chance on me. Working for Barbara was the beginning of my first mentoring relationship.

From age fourteen to my early twenties, I held many positions in and out of the hospitality industry. I was headstrong and sometimes let my emotions take over which can create career-limiting moves. While I was a hard worker, I did not stay in some jobs long because I did not agree with something, was impatient and had a limited perspective. I did not understand the concept of picking your battles, learning more about the operation than just my opinion and knowing when to communicate. These were hard lessons, but I got it!

I started college on a full scholarship and quit after one year. During my first year in college, I worked as a criminal bail-bonds person. I can assure you there were not any 18-year old females working in this role. I worked the 11 p.m. to 7 a.m, shift. I saw the worst of people and the best of people in this job. This experience had a profound impact on me.

During my freshman year in college, I had a good time working and partying, and my studies suffered. I also thought I knew everything because I was great at my job and did not believe I needed college. I quit everything and got a full-time job working at a hotel; first as a gift-shop clerk, then as the purchasing agent. I loved working at the hotel. That was true until I was age 22, and then I noticed everyone was getting promoted because they had a degree. Not having a degree was a problem because I knew I wanted a promotion.

At 22, the next job I had was working at the United States Post Office in the Houston downtown location. The reason I deviated from the hospitality industry this time was to please my grandfather. He had worked at the post office in a small town in Illinois and retired after forty years. He talked about working at the post office with so much pride. His experience was not my experience. I felt I was not utilizing my skills and knew my real passion was the hospitality industry. Looking back at this experience was exactly the motivation I needed to go back to college. I now had the motivation and drive to finish my degree. And yes, now I was paying my way. Did I tell you I have to learn things the hard way sometimes?

College the second time around was different. I was exposed to so many career paths in the hospitality industry that I did not know existed. There were so many great faculty members like Dean Gerald Lattin, Dr. John Bowen, Dr. Raymond Goodman, Dr. Clinton Rappole, and Don Smith, who taught at the University of Houston Hilton College and went out of their way for their students to help their hospitality careers.

It was not until I completed my bachelor's degree in Hotel and Restaurant Management that I settled on what I wanted to do; I knew I wanted to be a hotel general manager. I did not know any women who were hotel general managers at the time, but that did not stop me. I decided the best way to get there was to work in every department of the hotel to be competent. I had seen too many general managers who did not have depth in their role. I did not want to be like them. The other thing I noticed was many managers wanted their jobs to seem complicated and tried to exclude younger people like me from learning. I swore to myself that once I was in charge, I would work hard to simplify things for everyone to understand and use language to include people.

I know my "why" was to become the best example of an exceptional leader. I had only worked for one exceptional leader after almost 15 years of work experience, and I wanted to emulate her while being true to myself. It seems to me that exceptional leaders are rare.

I also believed earning an MBA would open new doors and opportunities for me, and it did. At the age of 29, I became a hotel general manager. I was the youngest female hotel manager in Houston at that time. I was thrilled. I intended to create a work environment where employees felt appreciated. The business model at that time was to take care of the guests. Truthfully that made no sense to me, as hotel guests are transient. I believed that if I focused on the hotel employees and they were happy and satisfied in their roles, the guests would be taken care of well. I continued to work hard, coach, and develop my employees and we achieved terrific results.

It is also true that there were many scary days where I was thrown into new situations and had to figure it out on my own. Some of those examples were basements flooding, electrical problems shutting down the elevator system with a one hundred percent occupancy, lack of a preventive maintenance system, a fire breaking out in the building next door, pipes breaking on occasion, employees stealing, and human-resource issues, from drugs to severe illness, etc. There were moments I thought I should have paid more attention to my hotel facility operations class when these problems appeared.

What served me best was remaining calm in the middle of the chaos, because at the end of the day, I knew I was responsible for each person in the hotel — employees and guests. I have created sayings for myself that I live by and they serve me well. One such saying is "Circumstances do not define me." This saying helps me see beyond what is happening now, so we do not lose focus and can get to the other side to achieve expected results.

I managed and served others the way I wanted to be treated. What I am most proud of is that many of these employees have stayed in touch with me after this many years.

After having served as a hotel general manager for several hotels, I earned the opportunity to work for Hilton Hotels Inc. First was the position as divisional manager for operations for twelve Hilton franchise properties and then as a divisional manager in marketing for fifty Hilton hotels. I loved every minute of it. My values fit with the Hilton culture. Hilton has high standards, has exceptional training, and holds their people accountable. I worked with some fantastic colleagues under the leadership of Eric Hilton, Yvonne Levine, David Conway, and the Southwest office staff.

I was the first woman divisional manager for the office hired and with it came a high sense of responsibility so other women could follow in my footsteps. I felt so blessed for all these opportunities I have been given, but in the back of my mind, I truly wanted to teach and give back to the profession that has given so much to me. In order to teach at the University level in my program area, a doctorate degree is required. I chose a doctorate in education specializing in curriculum and instruction, because it interested me. In order not to put too much pressure on myself, I thought well, I would apply and see what happens. I was accepted. I thought well, I would take one class and see if I can pass. I did. I excelled in my classes and finished my comps. During this time, we had to choose a dissertation advisor. We were told to choose wisely. I wanted the toughest instructor in the College of Education, Dr. Will Weber. I picked him because I believed that if I could meet his expectations during this time when it came to defending my dissertation, he would support me. That is precisely what Dr. Weber did. I wrote and defended my dissertation and graduated, summa cum laude.

I was so excited because now I had the degree, the experience, and the passion. Guess what? No one would hire me. All they saw was a hotel manager. It was frustrating, but I did not give up. After three years of applying for teaching jobs, I took a job in a private school as a business manager, hoping to build a bridge from one industry to another. I heard about this job from one of my classmates, Deb, in graduate school. Your network is vital in these types of situations.

About the time I was coming up on one year of working at the private school, something else happened. My best friend, Dan Prosser, told me about a personal development course I should register for, and so I did in May of 1993. The company was Landmark Education. I took the entire curriculum for living. I can honestly say it has been life-changing. Through the questioning process, it opened me up to my blind spots and transformed my results in all areas of my life.

Within a week of completing the first-weekend course, Barbara McDonald and Yvonne Levine told me about a new culinary school opening at The Art Institute of Houston, and they suggested I apply. Michael Nenes, the Culinary Director, took a chance on me as a part-time instructor. He did this in large part because of my doctorate, my culinary-related dissertation, hospitality experience, and passion for teaching.

Now, remember I was at the top of my career in the hospitality industry, earning an excellent salary. I knew that when I transitioned into higher education, I would take a drastic cut in pay. I was starting at the bottom, but I knew my desire and work ethic would pay off.

I accepted this opportunity of a part-time teaching position at a college where I could use my academic degree and my hospitality experience; it was a dream come true. I soon became a full-time faculty member. Within two years I was promoted to the position of the College Dean because of my past substantial administrative experience. I was not looking to get promoted. I loved teaching, and I enjoyed my students. The administration approached me about becoming the Dean. I was contacted about the new position in large part due to my volunteering to take on projects in other departments and chair highly visible committees. I got noticed! That is the good and bad news.

I struggled with the new job. I was not ready. One day I am a faculty member, the next day I am the Dean. It was wrought with all kinds of challenges if you know the higher education hierarchy. Specifically, one day I was the employee in the culinary department with a supervisor and the next day I was the supervisor over my supervisor. It was awkward. The truth is that the program directors knew I did not have the answers, but they granted me grace. I could not pretend I knew the answers. They would ask me questions, and I would have to research and get back with them, which I did. My mentor in this situation was Dr. Michael Maki who helped me tremendously as he had held the role previously. You might find yourself in a similar situation. Let's say you get promoted, and now you are managing your peers. It is tricky. I highly recommend hiring a business coach or having a mentor who can help you navigate your new role successfully.

Besides, three days before I stepped into this role, my brother died. I thought I would throw myself into the job and learn as much as I could, as quickly as possible. It was rough. In some ways, it was good I had such a challenging position, with less time to think about the loss of my brother. The truth is that is not how grief works. I felt like I was living inside a marshmallow. I could see and hear everyone, but I could not connect with them, if that makes sense. You cannot ignore grief, and I should not have taken the job. The reality is that for a long time, I was not there emotionally, but produced tactical results. I persevered but did not prosper. Once I worked through the grief, I realized what was important in life. It was the best lesson my brother could have taught me. I found new compassion for people. I felt a deeper connection with everyone personally and professionally. I elevated my emotional intelligence. No one knows how losing someone will affect them and how long the grieving process will take. I think it also helped me help others when they experienced death in their family to give them time to heal and not rush them. My brother gave me the gift of grace.

Two years later, I was tapped for an Assistant Vice President (AVP) corporate position, out of state, overseeing academic operations for all the schools in the division. Within a short period of accepting this new role in Pittsburgh, the corporation posted my dream job of faculty development in 1997. I knew I could not apply for the job since I had just accepted the operations role. There were company rules set up for not being able to transfer to another position for at least a year. I was disappointed, of course, but took advantage of learning the good, bad, and ugly of every institution operation we had so I could help make a difference.

Three years later, the College President position was posted for the Houston location, my hometown. I received a lot of encouragement to apply, and I did. Armed with seven years of experience in a variety of roles for the same company, and eight interviews later, I was given the position of the College President by the Corporation and Board of Trustees. I was returning to Houston as the President, and yet I had some concerns, as this was the location where I had taken the Dean of Education position when my brother had died. On my first day back on campus, I dealt with the elephant in the room. I knew individual faculty and staff did not care for me or even trust me from my history and did not feel the connection to me. I held an all-employee town hall meeting, my first day back on campus. I remember it like it was yesterday. I remember telling them how excited I was to have been given the opportunity to lead this extraordinary campus. It is where my heart was and where I felt like I had found my home in higher education. I told them that I had changed and learned a lot over the past three years. I shared that I was sure they had grown and changed as well. I then said I was looking forward to getting to know them and we would learn from each other in a new way. This meeting was the beginning step in rebuilding trust. I worked diligently, and I am proud to say, I still consider each person on the team to be a lifetime friend.

Also, I hired an executive business coach on my own to make sure

I would be successful in my new role. I believe that coaches can give you a different perspective, so you can consider what is best for you and the organization. My personal experience is that excellent coaches build in accountability and help you set aside your own opinions to achieve organizational results in a faster time frame.

Every organization is different — the culture, the people, the mission, vision, and values. I remember from my first day as a part-time college instructor; I felt like I belonged when I walked in the building. It was a great feeling. Remember, while the company is interviewing you for a position, you also need to consider whether it is an organization where you would fit in and like to work as part of your career journey. The fit is essential when you are considering working for an organization or if you already work for an organization.

I learned this first hand in one of my bad hiring decisions. Every organization has their hiring process. Our process was a resume screen, an initial phone interview, group panel interview, an interview with the Executive Committee and the final interview with me. The candidate interviewed well and checked all our boxes. The candidate was hired. I met with her on her first day, and within two hours, I knew we had made a terrible mistake. She honestly did not fit into our culture. It was a painful and costly mistake. What I learned from the experience is that you look for experience, credentials, behaviors, skills, traits, and attitude — and most importantly, do not forget fit. While she was technically competent, she did not possess emotional intelligence, creativity, depth, energy, or the ability to think outside the box. We followed due process and gave her every opportunity to become successful, but she was not coachable. Eventually, I had to terminate her. Terminations are always painful for both parties, and this was especially true in this situation.

I served as President of the College until 2005 when my dream job was reposted for VP of Faculty Development in Pittsburgh. I finally had the chance to interview. There were some amazingly qualified faculty development directors in our company. I did not believe I was a shoo-in for the job. Some people in the company could not understand why a College President would want to take this type of position. To others in the company this VP position seemed like a lateral move or a step down, but then they did not know my "why."

My "why" was simple; I wanted to help and make a difference for others. Ask any new teacher or even those who have been teaching for awhile; teaching is hard. Teaching is challenging. Teaching is rewarding.

I remember that when I first started teaching, it was hard. I had the academic credentials, the industry experience, but no idea about the art and science of teaching. I went on a mission to perfect my craft in teaching and engaging students. Once I learned how to teach effectively, I wanted to share what I had learned with others. I wanted to engage our faculty to make teaching easier. I wanted to demonstrate to our faculty what they could achieve without years of trial and error and student learning suffering in the meantime. I wanted to provide training and development that was practical and meaningful. My goal was to make the teaching pathway more natural, more fun, and fulfilling. I wanted our students to experience exceptional teaching and learning. Faculty development, coaching, and mentoring is my purpose.

Soon the day came for me to fly back to Pittsburgh to interview for the VP of Faculty Development position. During the interview, I handed my hiring manager a three-year strategic plan I had created for the faculty development. He said I did not have to create a plan. I said "Yes, I did. I did it for you and me." I told him the VP of Faculty Development was a highly visible position, and many leaders would be asking him what the return on investment was and expected deliverables for having someone in this position. I was honored to be selected; I stayed in the role for the next five years.

I began my role as VP of Faculty Development. One of the best pieces of advice I received from several senior-level managers was to spend the first thirty days of the job learning and asking questions. Over the course of the next thirty days, I held conversations with a cross-section of one hundred of our company employees. I surveyed all faculty. Armed with a lot of data, I recrafted my three-year strategic plan. The first year was dedicated to building a mandatory faculty orientation program for new faculty members. Also, the new faculty was expected to complete five introductory art-of-teaching modules. These programs could be delivered face to face or online. The second year was dedicated to our senior and most experienced faculty members. I called it the "gold" series to respect and enhance their teaching and thinking. The third-year filled in the gaps between the beginning and very experienced teacher workshops. We created fifteen workshops for the campus locations. Also, we created a "Train the Trainer" program for each campus to be able to deliver the material.

The fourth year expanded to the three other divisions of the company, which was programmatically very different. The highlight of that year was developing a specialized, comprehensive faculty nursing program. When I started working on this, I had no background in nursing. I did extensive research, talked to all the nursing directors, read books, and sat in nursing classes. I then developed the program. Before I launched the program, I held a three-day retreat for nursing directors. At the conclusion of the retreat, several nursing directors asked if I was a nurse. What a compliment! I was so honored. I said I was not a trained nurse but was committed to making the training practical with real nursing examples.

My fifth year in the faculty development role was even better. As I have mentioned, my background was in the hospitality industry. I was asked to design a highly specialized culinary faculty development program for the faculty members who taught our international cuisine classes. The corporate Culinary Director had a vision, and he put it into place. He wanted the faculty members of each cuisine to be taught by a Master Chef in that cuisine for two days. This would provide a consistent and specialized training experience. On the third day of each of these trainings, I was asked to come in and demonstrate to the faculty how they would apply what they had learned in the lab. Talk about challenging and exhilarating! Again, this required hours of research, talking to each Master Chef and the corporate Culinary Director of desired outcomes. At the conclusion of these five years, I believed that I had created and delivered a sustainable program. I began thinking it might be time for someone else to take my place.

In the meantime, what you don't know is that the person the company hired back in 1997 for the VP of Faculty Development had failed miserably. It was a loss for everyone. The company kept the position open for at least five years before reposting. Looking back at it now, if I had taken the job in 1997, I would have failed miserably. I did not have enough experience, and I could not have helped all of the faculty who depended on me. We don't always know why things happen the way they do at the time, but most of the time it is revealed to us later.

As the VP of Faculty Development, I wanted to be a good role model for the faculty, so I went back to college to earn another graduate degree – this time in instructional design and entirely online. I wanted to be a good role model because we were asking our faculty to obtain higher academic credentials, while they were teaching, working and caring for families. I know we were asking a lot, but it was required. Education is always changing, I needed the skill-set, and wanted to be current with online and blended learning. Before this, my previous education experience had been at traditional universities.

After having spent seventeen years with one company, it was time for a change. The last five years in my dream job kept me on the road, traveling seventy-five percent of the year. I have a family, and I missed them very much. I resigned and decided to take stock of my life. There was no rush, but it was the first time since I was fourteen years old that I did not have a job. A recruiter called me and asked me to interview at a local college for a President position. I did. They hired me very quickly. I rushed to a decision, and it was a mistake. I knew on the first day when I walked into the college I did not fit the culture. I worked very hard but within six months I knew I could not change the culture; I tried, but senior management had no interest in doing the right thing. I am not proud of this, but I learned a lot about myself, what I believe in, what I value, and what I stand for in higher education. I resigned, and this time took the time I needed to reflect.

What did I know at this point? I knew I wanted to work in Houston. I knew I loved higher education. I knew I had to work for a company that held culture, mission, vision, and values in high esteem. I wanted to work for a company that valued their employees at all levels. I missed being on campus. There is particular energy with the faculty, staff and the students. I love building teams and coaching people to excel in their careers. I was not looking but once again because of my network, I was contacted by a former colleague, Dr. Maki, who told me about a University President position available in Houston. I applied and was given the opportunity to lead this campus for the next six years. We created a unique culture and a University that students enjoyed attending and employees looked forward to coming to work. At the end of six years, the campus transitioned from brick and mortar to fully online, resulting in all of us losing our positions. As a result, it was time for a new beginning.

In 2015, I opened a consulting business with a partner, John Morales. We specialized in faculty development, process improvement, business consulting, and leadership coaching. It is rewarding work because we believe in helping individuals and organizations develop their talent pool while maximizing revenue and retention goals. From the beginning, John suggested I write a book, and my response was always the same. "I am never going to write a book." I would say, I love teaching, coaching, facilitating workshops and speaking. Well, in 2016, I had to reexamine my mindset. While I pride myself on having a growth mindset, this was one area where I was fixed. Where did that fixed or negative mindset come from?

In October, 2016, my church held a writing workshop by Tom Bird and from that one event, I have written three books and have become a best-selling author. My first book is titled *Did I Say Never?* (How appropriate!) My second book is titled *52 Weeks to Exceptional Leadership*. I did not do this alone. I owe my writing and publishing success to Tom Bird, John Hodgkinson, and Denise Cassino. It takes a team of professionals to help you achieve your dreams.

You are reading my third book, called Promotion *Protocol: Unlock the Secrets of Promotability and Career Success*. The point is that if I had not been willing to look at myself and assessing my negative thoughts about writing, none of this would have ever happened. If my business partner had not pushed me, this writing career would not have happened. I believe that by my sharing my story, you can investigate your life and see where your "never" lives. If you are willing, this will open you up to new possibilities in your life. I believe in you. We can do this together if you allow me to take you on this career journey.

Throughout my career, I found it very important to stay current. For me, it meant a formal education, taking personal development courses to discover my blind spots, reading, listening, having mentors and hiring a business coach.

I also am a student of life. I like to put myself in challenging situations to see if I can accomplish them. Whether it be yoga, weight training, writing, dancing, cooking, or traveling internationally, every opportunity is a growth experience; a chance to learn; expand my mind and add depth.

It is my desire that after you read my story you see parts of yourself in it. As I have revealed my story, I hope you can feel my energy, authenticity, and passion for helping others. My background is eclectic and was not a straight line. I was impatient, but I figured it out, with a lot of help from mentors and coaches.

I know if you are willing to self-assess your strengths and developmental areas, you can accomplish anything you put your mind toward achieving.

Before we begin the self-assessment, let's examine the reality of the workplace, why you might not have been promoted, your motivation, the keys to being promoted, the characteristics of becoming a high-potential candidate, your mindset and how we can provide a pathway going forward.

THE REALITY OF THE WORKPLACE TODAY

All this sounds great — but here is the reality. Senior leaders today have competing priorities, the pressure to increase revenue, achieve the metrics, meet impossible deadlines, in high-stress positions, and more responsibility with fewer resources. They lack the time to adequately coach and develop employees in the way they wish.

The US Bureau of Labor Statistics (2018) states we have the following numbers in the workplace: 56 million millennials, 53 million generation Xers, and 41 million baby boomers. Baby boomers are retiring faster than the next generation can replace them in experience readiness. Senior leaders recognize they have talented people working for them but while they have the desire to develop them, they do not have the time to devote to coaching and mentoring. Sending the employee to another training course is not the solution, either.

So, what is the answer? What if we could provide you with a framework for your weekly coaching meetings? What if your employee would start with a self-assessment to begin to see how these traits can be cultivated? What if we gave the supervisor a set of coaching questions each week? What if both the employee and the supervisor could come to the meeting both knowing what the questions would be for the next twenty-six weeks? The purpose would be to save time, create a collaborative environment, and have a sense of shared expectations. This book is that solution. So let's get started.

As the supervisor, schedule the weekly coaching meetings. There must be a consistent framework for setting up coaching, accountability, and feedback. Commit to this schedule. Have an agenda. Take notes. These meetings can be scheduled face-to-face, on the phone, or through digital technology. For the supervisor and employee read the trait starting with "A" first. The employee should come prepared for the meeting with the weekly self-assessment answers written out in whatever media you prefer. Before we start on this journey, let's look at why employees might not be getting promotions. I know if you are willing to self-assess your strengths and developmental areas, you can accomplish anything you put your mind toward achieving.

Before we begin the self-assessment, let's examine the reality of the workplace, why you might not have been promoted, your motivation, the keys to being promoted, the characteristics of becoming a high-potential candidate, your mindset and how we can provide a pathway going forward.

Promotion Protocol

EVER WONDER WHY YOU ARE NOT GETTING PROMOTED?

You might have been with your company six months or a few years, and then you see a position for which you want to apply, so you apply, and actually, are given an opportunity to interview. You are professionally dressed, prepared with a digital presentation, and answered all the questions from the panel. You are sure you got the promotion.

Within a few weeks, you are notified that you did not get the promotion. You really cannot understand this. You begin thinking the people at this company do not like you. It almost becomes self-fulfilling. You start demonstrating negative behaviors, a bad attitude, complaining, and you possibly even begin to look for a new job outside of the company. Think again.

Let's look at this objectively. Let's say there is only one open position; four internal candidates and several external candidates are applying for the same job. Do the math. If the opportunity is given to an internal candidate, obviously three employees will not be given this opportunity. I hope you work for a company that would be willing to tell you why you were not selected, so you can begin to work on those areas. It is also possible that you work for a company that does not share this type of feedback. Well, if that is the case, then you can ask the hiring manager for specific feedback with the idea in mind to improve any shortcomings.

Make an appointment with the hiring manager. Tell them you want to stay with the company, improve your skill set and be promoted in the future. Ask if they would be willing to share specific areas where you did well and areas that needed improvement. Hopefully, they will give constructive feedback. Listen. Do not argue, justify, or defend. Just because you think you nailed the interview on that day does not mean you are getting the promotion. So, learn from this, as I believe you will have an opportunity again.

As a senior hiring manager in my organization, I have seen these situations time and time again. What I often say to disheartened candidates is this: "If you want to be promoted, you must be the best candidate for the position, not just for the best interview or the day." Just because you were outstanding on this day, the truth is you have to be twice as good as any external candidate. Here is why. We have had lots of time to see your performance in your current role. If you have not been responsible, not met deadlines, not dressed appropriately, nor have been a valued contributor, we are more likely to take a chance on someone who has proven themselves or take a chance on an external candidate, rather than hire mediocrity. We know the good, the bad, and the ugly about you. You cannot redeem yourself in one interview and promise things will dramatically change. I know this is harsh! Let me tell you how it is, so next time you have a real opportunity for that promotion. **Let me give you three real examples:**

The first one is a graduate student of mine. English is not his first language. He struggled to speak and write in English. He had been a full-time employee for six years with a well-known company in the city. He longed for a management position. He had tried several times and was denied. Coincidentally, I had heard the owner of his company speak at a citywide forum on today's workforce and what he valued in his employees and organization. He said it is all about communication for promotability in his organization. One night before class started, this graduate student came in and was complaining about his company and how he did not get the promotion and how they did not appreciate him. I mentioned I had heard the owner talking about this very subject. I told him he needed to improve his communication skills if he wanted to move into management. His response was: "No, that can't be it." OK, it is his future. I believe this response to the feedback can be called denial.

The second example is of a young woman who worked in my organization. She applied for a position and assumed she got it. While I was not the hiring manager, I was on the panel. She did a great job in the interview, but we did not feel her skill set was the right one, and she was missing essential experience. We ended up hiring an external candidate. I took particular time to sit with her and explain to her that she was not ready right now for this position but possibly sometime in the future. I knew she was very disappointed. I asked her if she would be able to come to work with a positive attitude and be willing to learn from the new person. She said she would. The reality is she did not. Her work performance fell off, she started complaining, and started to hang around with one or two other negative people who blamed others for their situations. It was toxic. She eventually left the organization and unfortunately has not found her dream position. She felt she was entitled to the promotion and her response to feedback was jealousy, frustration, and anger.

The third example is interesting. We had a female international employee who was given an opportunity to become a manager. We believed she had the skill set, but we recognized she had no prior management experience. While she had the desire for the position, she found it very hard to relate to the American workforce at times. We were willing to take a chance on her. Many people mentored her, but she failed in her first year to make those connections. She was too task-oriented rather than relationship-oriented. When the time came to conduct her annual review, her supervisor was very direct. While this new manager was highly intelligent, she lacked in many vital areas. She received a less-than-satisfactory performance evaluation. This manager went home crushed. She took the feedback. She reflected. It took her about a week to think through it all and devise a plan. She sought out critical managers in the organization to learn how she came across and how she could improve without complaining. Then she went to work on herself. The next year she received an excellent performance evaluation. It was so gratifying to see. Everyone celebrated with her.

Not surprisingly, she went on to earn further promotions and stretch herself. Her response to this example was constructive. It is all about how you handle it!

The next time you apply for a promotion, think about these examples. Think about who you are, and who you want to be. Think about the combination of knowledge, skills, attitude, and traits you bring to the position. Think about how you are qualified and if are you ready. So, before you apply for a promotion, let's get serious and do some critical thinking.

WHAT IS YOUR MOTIVATION FOR A PROMOTION?

Have you thought about the "why" you want to be promoted? You need to be prepared to answer this question. Consider doing a career map where you map out your goals, purpose, and practice before you apply for the position. Your "why" answer will serve you and propel you when you are promoted and must get through those challenging and stressful days.

You may have personal reasons that are driving you for that promotion. You may want to become more financially secure rather than living paycheck to paycheck. You might want to be a positive role model for your family and crave the recognition. You may be looking to expand the scope of your work and take on more diverse projects. You might have professional reasons for wanting a promotion. You might want to take on the challenge of a new job instead of the one you have. You may want to lead a team of people and make a more significant contribution to the company.

You might have a plan to retire earlier than your friends, and you plan to accept more and more challenging projects to ensure it happens. You might want to be known as the problem solver in your company and get to the root cause and provide solutions. Know your reason. Once again, you must be ready to answer this question when you are interviewed.

You must know the reasons that are propelling you to seek a promotion. Simon Sinek, author of *Start with Why*, (2011), is known for asking "What is your why?" It is an essential concept in leadership and business. Your answer will give insight into what inspires you and propels you to want to go forward. It will sustain you. According to Sinek, starting with "why" is what separates great companies from good companies because the great ones begin with "why," rather than what or how. If you know your "why," it will help inspire you to take action. Your "why" may be personal or professional, or a combination of both. I recommend watching the *How Great Leaders Inspire Action* by Simon Sinek. Watch his TedTalk on YouTube to appreciate his brilliance and begin to better understand your "why." Once you do that, let's examine characteristics of high potential employees.

CHARACTERISTICS OF HIGH POTENTIAL CANDIDATES

Have you ever heard of the term "high potential?" It is a term used in performance evaluation systems to describe employees that have the potential and ability to lead, regardless of whether they are currently in a leadership role. According to Greg Bungay, performance accelerator coach, (2015), "great employees are reliable, accountable, proactive, and have high potential" (p. 2). Think about people you work with and who you think are high potential. So, let's break it down.

According to Justin Reynolds, consultant and freelance writer, (Mar 1, 2017), "High-potential employees are incredibly talented, are consistent, and are good at their job" (p. 1). Know what your talents are. Being consistent at work is not "sometimes" or on days "when you feel like it," it is an everyday trait. Being good at your job is knowing every aspect so you can deliver the results expected. I know first-hand there are many parts of every job I have had and enjoyed. I can also say there are parts of every job I do not care for and yet it was imperative for me to learn those parts and not shy away. What you don't know will hurt you in your career.

Great employees jump in and solve problems. They do not sit around and wait. They do whatever it takes. They take the initiative. For example, you might have seen this person as they volunteer or emerge as a leader on a project or committee. No one gave them a title; they merely emerged as a leader to solve problems. They bring new energy to the position and share ideas with leadership. They design their career path and seek out new opportunities. The high-potential employees talk to their manager and together work on a career development plan. Now when you are younger in your career, this can be daunting to think about having these conversations, but is a critical trait to master.

The great employees continue to develop their skills, seek knowledge, and possess a positive attitude. Developing skills is not just isolated to the actual job but rather a holistic development of skills. High-potentials are never satisfied with the status quo. They continue to learn and yearn for more for themselves and the organization. For me, I was always impatient. I wanted things yesterday, so I understand the desire to get promoted. I also appreciate the desire that if it does not happen in your timeline, there is a personal tendency to want to quit and get another job. Before you make the change, think about how you can create new opportunities for yourself in the company, regardless of title. If you start solving problems, you will get noticed.

These great employees are authentic, have depth, have energy, are unique, and think outside of the box. I call this trait "eclectic." You might not be able to describe it, but you know it when you see it.

The high-potentials' soft skills, especially communications skills, are excellent. Soft skills can be learned. Examples of soft skills are communication, teamwork, problem-solving, integrity, and professional dress. They know when to speak up in meetings and when to dial it down. They know when to pick their battles. I know from first-hand experience, learning this lesson the hard way. Take your passion and know when to use it. Said another way, these remarkable employees are flexible and not positional. They do not complain in public. They respect others and earn people's trust by keeping their word. You can count on them. They have integrity. They collaborate and deliver the result. While they are great communicators, they are open to feedback. They do not always have to be right. They do not have to have the last word on every subject. They come to work with a positive attitude and are consistent.

Does this description of a great employee have you wanting to work with someone like this? Is that someone YOU? Do you possess these characteristics? Tell the truth.

KEYS TO BEING PROMOTED – SURVEY SAID

What are these exceptional leadership traits? What are the keys? What is the pathway? In preparation for this book, I created an online focus group. It was made up of young professionals and senior leaders. I asked several questions related to leadership traits and promotability. As the survey results came in, I thought, oh no, this couldn't be. I was expecting pretty much to have a consensus of answers. What I found instead was there is a considerable gap. Baby boomers had their ideas. Gen Xers had their opinions. Millennials had a different set of responses. The responses from our online focus group mirrored Anne Liotta's work. Anne Liotta is a generational speaker, author and expert in the field. Let's break it down.

Overall, our research and experience tell us that our baby boomer leaders have a vision of the big picture. They have a strength of character, called integrity and authenticity. They have a drive and resilience. They have initiative. They are highly consistent, competent, and produce results and rewards. Baby boomers tend to see career pathways as a ladder that must be climbed. They love data, taking notes, and follow-up and follow-through. They possess exceptional presentation and communication skills, both verbal and non-verbal. They like face-to-face meetings, titles, and a career hierarchy. They are relationship-focused to build teams and a healthy culture. Baby boomers are not as technology fluent as other generations. Another problem is that baby boomers are retiring in large numbers or leaving the workplace to enjoy their lives. The problem is that many baby boomers see career growth and promotion opportunities as successive and other generations do not see it that way. Baby boomers may not be open to learning new ways of doing things because their experience gets in the way. So here is another gap.

Generation Xer's prefer 20-minute meetings; sort of like a Ted-Talk: business first, and brevity according to Liotta (2012). They want you to lead with "what is in it for me" and state the value up front. In my experience as a college professor, almost all adult students feel the same way and want to know the "WIIFM." Generation Xer's hate to waste time. Give them the timeline, the budget, and the deliverables and they are good to go. They value competence and do not want to be micromanaged.

Millennials value coaching and mentoring. In general, this generation values technology, social media, podcasts, smartphones, web-based learning, and texting because they grew up with it (Liotta, 2012, p. 170). They love doing their own research because they can either use Google©, go to YouTube© or find what they need online. Millennials love collaboration, working in groups, and acknowledgment for their effort. They learn super-fast, and they dive into learning new things. They like working with supervisors who appreciate them and their efforts.

Once I stepped back, I realized this is the real opportunity to bridge the leadership gap and expectations. Let's capitalize on the gifts of each generation and bridge the differences. There are considerable experience, expectations, and leadership gaps we must fill quickly but with a quality approach. Anne Liotta states that it is critical for all leaders to be generational savvy (2012, p. 178). She goes on to further explain that across generations, remember this:

>"Feedback is key.
>Social media is mission-critical to communication.
>Multitasking is a way of life.
>Dress code needs a purpose.
>Careers are not about titles but knowledge and skills.
>What motivates you, does not motivate others, so ask."

I say, coaching is the new approach for a new generation and the time is now.

THE SOLUTION

The solution is this book! It is a guide to help you as the coach. It will help you mentor the talent in your organization. It will help you bridge the leadership gap and leave a legacy. It will help change the workplace reality of today, which is bleak. If this process is followed, the future of the workplace becomes one of the possibilities. The solution is this book if you are the employee, as it gives you a place to start down your promotion pathway.

One of the most challenging jobs of a supervisor is to find the right person for the position. As a supervisor or coach, you want to be able to tap into the skills, knowledge, aptitude, and passion of the individual that match the position. Too many times a person takes a job or applies for something without giving it enough thought. Too many times a hiring manager does not take the time to find the right candidate and hires a warm body, due to lack of time or pressure. I can assure you, you will pay for that decision many times over. So, take the time to find the right person the first time.

But let's assume you are great at finding the right people to start with your organization. How will you keep them? The generation at work today expects coaching and mentoring. Is that you? If that is not your principal strength, this book is a solution for you.

As the supervisor or coach, what leadership traits do you value? How can you develop a list of shared leadership traits for your team members? What do you value? What does your organization value? How can we create shared expectations with your team? How can you as the supervisor become a leadership coach? How can you develop the talent in your organization? How can you build your skills as a coach?

For the employee, what traits do you value? How would you like to be coached? How can you demonstrate you are a high-potential? Given what you have read so far, what possibilities do you see for your career and the organization? Where do you see you need to grow and develop? What motivates you? Before we dive into the Self-Assessment Guide and weekly coaching questions, let's see if you are ready.

The intention of the **Getting to Know You Guide** is for the employee to answer these questions before meeting with the coach or supervisor for the initial meeting. It helps set the stage for engaging in meaningful dialogue. As the coach or supervisor, have the employee fill out the Getting to Know You Guide before your next meeting. Ideally, it would be your initial meeting.

GETTING TO KNOW YOU GUIDE

Name:
Position:
Time-frame employed at the company:

Before we get started, let's get to know each other. We need to examine if you are in a growth mindset and want to take on being promoted and becoming a leader. By answering each of these questions, you will begin to examine your skills, traits, competencies, and abilities before using the self-assessment guide for each of the 26 traits.

What do you value?

What motivates you?

At the completion of the twenty-six weeks, what do you want to accomplish?

What do you want to achieve in your role?

In what time-frame?

What are the deliverables?

What do you think are the three priorities in your role?

What concerns you?

What type of support do you need?

What are your gifts?
____ Emotional Intelligence
____ Soft Skills
____ Intellectual
____ Creative
____ Relationships
____ Organized
____ Visionary
____ Technology
____ Other

How do you learn best?
____ Auditory
____ Visual
____ Tactile-Kinesthetic

What are three of your weaknesses?
a.
b.
c.

What is your personality style?

What is your preferred method of communication?

What self-assessments have you taken? Describe.

What do you do for your health and well-being?

What are some of your hobbies?

How do you solve problems?

What assistance do you need in overcoming obstacles?

What non-profit organizations (causes) do you support?

What were the last three books you read?

What podcasts do you listen to?

What is one of your favorite YouTube videos?

How do you want to be coached?

Thank you for completing the Getting to Know You Guide.

SELF-ASSESSMENT INVENTORY INSTRUCTIONS

What if we created a win-win situation? Let's begin by starting the self-assessment inventory. Please take it before you apply for the next promotion; self-assess. Let's get started.

If you are the employee and are reading this to improve your chances of getting promoted, please begin by completing the self-assessment. In the first column, rate yourself in each category from 1 to 10; 1 being poor and 10 being excellent. Do not skip any of the twenty-six categories. Save the second column for your weekly coaching meetings.

If you are the supervisor, schedule weekly coaching meetings. Read through the questions before you meet with the employee, so you have a sense of where you want to take the conversation. Feel free to enhance the questions based on your company's culture and environment. This approach will help you mentor a new generation of aspiring leaders. Know that by using this approach you are leaving a legacy for our high-potentials to step into their future.

SELF-ASSESSMENT INVENTORY

ABC's of Promotability	Plan to Improve/Resources Utilized
Rate Yourself 1-10. 1 Being Poor, 10 Being Excellent.	
1 2 3 4 5 6 7 8 9 10 Attitude	
1 2 3 4 5 6 7 8 9 10 Brand	
1 2 3 4 5 6 7 8 9 10 Communication	
1 2 3 4 5 6 7 8 9 10 Depth	
1 2 3 4 5 6 7 8 9 10 Energy	
1 2 3 4 5 6 7 8 9 10 Focus	
1 2 3 4 5 6 7 8 9 10 Gratitude	

ABC's of Promotability	Plan to Improve/Resources Utilized
Rate Yourself 1-10. 1 Being Poor, 10 Being Excellent.	
1 2 3 4 5 6 7 8 9 10 Habits	
1 2 3 4 5 6 7 8 9 10 Integrity	
1 2 3 4 5 6 7 8 9 10 Jaded	
1 2 3 4 5 6 7 8 9 10 Knowledgeable	
1 2 3 4 5 6 7 8 9 10 Life-Long Learner	
1 2 3 4 5 6 7 8 9 10 Mindset	
1 2 3 4 5 6 7 8 9 10 Network	
1 2 3 4 5 6 7 8 9 10 Opportunity	
1 2 3 4 5 6 7 8 9 10 Problem Solver	
1 2 3 4 5 6 7 8 9 10 Question	

ABC's of Promotability	Plan to Improve/Resources Utilized
Rate Yourself 1-10. 1 Being Poor, 10 Being Excellent.	
1 2 3 4 5 6 7 8 9 10 Responsibility	
1 2 3 4 5 6 7 8 9 10 Self-Awareness	
1 2 3 4 5 6 7 8 9 10 Thank You	
1 2 3 4 5 6 7 8 9 10 Unique	
1 2 3 4 5 6 7 8 9 10 Vision	
1 2 3 4 5 6 7 8 9 10 White Lies	
1 2 3 4 5 6 7 8 9 10 X-Factor	
1 2 3 4 5 6 7 8 9 10 Yearning	
1 2 3 4 5 6 7 8 9 10 Zone	

THE SOLUTION FOR LEADERS AND THE NEW GENERATION OF ASPIRING LEADERS

If certain leadership traits can be agreed upon, can we have a common ground for shared expectations? How can the supervisor indeed become a coach? How can the employee be mentored? How can the employee demonstrate they are a high-potential? What if we created a Win-Win? Let's start with our aspiring leaders. It is time to take the self-assessment and begin our journey together.

Before You Apply for a Promotion, take the Self-Awareness Inventory. So, let's make the promotion path real! Let's examine why you might not be getting that promotion. I have created a guide to work on specific traits to enhance promotion opportunities. I call them the ABC's for promotability.

Let's get started. Review the list of tips. How well did you do?

What areas could be improved? Create an improvement plan. Start NOW! That promotion could come sooner than you think.

The framework of this book is to set up weekly coaching meetings. The employee should read and answer all the self-assessment questions starting in week one with the letter A-Attitude. This is the prep work for the coaching meeting. The coach or supervisor will come to the meeting having reviewed the coaching questions. Many of the questions each week will be similar. Both sets are questions are written out for transparency purposes so there are no surprises for either party. The coach always has the flexibility to add or modify the questions based on the organization, and culture.

KIM NUGENT

ATTITUDE

> " A positive attitude gives you power over your circumstances instead of allowing your circumstances to have power over you.
>
> — Joyce Meyer

A IS FOR ATTITUDE

How important do you think having a positive and professional attitude at work is? What is your attitude each day when you arrive at work? What about throughout the day? Do people like to be around you? Do you bring a positive outlook to the workspace, or do people avoid you? Do you bring down the team? Do people make excuses for you, such as saying, "Well that is just the way he is" and try and avoid you? Are you an energy drain on the team? Don't be a Debbie Downer or a Ned Know It All.

Jon Gordon wrote an article called "How to Deal with Energy Vampires" after writing his book *The Energy Bus*. The point is you do not want to be known in your company as an energy vampire. A person who sucks the air out of the room. You feel bored, overwhelmed, and frustrated by them. These people exist. Make sure you are not one of them. Remember, bad attitudes are contagious, and so are good ones. How would people you work with describe your attitude?

According to the dictionary, the definition of attitude is a way of thinking or feeling expressed through behaviors. Attitude can be expressed in a variety of ways such as job satisfaction, productivity, innovation, respect, helpfulness, and overall morale within the department.

Attitude is fundamental to your career success. It is a social "soft skill." There are many excellent assessments online that you could take to form a baseline if you do not feel you are as self-aware as you would like to be. Assessments can include career, communication, mindset, personality, attitude, emotional intelligence, leadership skills, etc. We all have blind spots, so the more you begin to uncover yours and take action steps to improve, the more confident and more promotable you become. Start out each day with a gratitude journal or positive meditation or affirmations. The more consistent you are with starting each day like this, the more your attitude will improve. Taking small steps each day creates more significant attitude opportunities. Once you find the beauty in the little things, your universe seems to expand in higher proportion. Surround yourself with positive people. Don't you love being around positive people? I know positive people inspire and motivate me. They make me smile. Do you make others smile?

Do good work without expecting anything in return. Be willing to forgive. Learn from your mistakes and do not beat yourself up mentally. When you make a mistake, get in the habit of thinking through what you learned and then move on. Do not dwell on negative things, people, or conversations. I believe part of my professional success is I do not dwell on problems. I get into action, and work towards a solution. My advice is get into action and a change in attitude will follow.

John C. Maxwell wrote a book, titled *Attitude 101: What Every Leader Needs to Know*. This book is a practical guide and a great place to start examining your thoughts, feelings, and behaviors at work. You can determine your circumstances by maintaining a positive attitude. You can energize the team. You can take your first step toward leadership by improving your attitude at work, with family, and friends. It starts with you, attitude is a choice.

Self-Assessment Questions

Question:
How self-aware are you?

Response:

Question:
Have you ever taken an attitude assessment? Have you ever had a 360-degree performance assessment in your career? If yes, what did it reveal?

Response:

Question:

If you were to ask your peers about your attitude, what would they say? Interview 3 to 5 people you trust that will give you direct feedback about your attitude.

Response:

Question:

What would your supervisor say regarding your attitude? If you do not know, ask.

Response:

Question:

If you have direct reports, what would they say?

Response:

Question:

What would your family say about your attitude?

Response:

Question:
When you hit a roadblock at work, how do you handle it?

Response:

Question:
Do you feel like you are resilient? If yes, give an example.

Response:

Question:
In what area do you think you excel?

Response:

Question:
What is one area in which you could improve your attitude?

Response:

Question:
What is one action step you can take to improve in this area?

Response:

Question:
How will you know you are making progress?

Response:

Coach/Mentor Questions

Q: Describe your attitude self-assessment.

Response:

Q: Did you ask others for feedback about your attitude?

Response:

Q: Did you learn anything new?

Response:

Q: Did any comments surprise you?

Response:

Q: What is one action step you can take to improve your attitude?
Response:

Q: How will you measure your improvement in this area?
Response:

Q: How can I support you?
Response:

Promotion Protocol

KIM NUGENT

BRAND

> " Your brand is what people say about you when you are not in the room.
> — Jeff Bezos, Amazon

B IS FOR BRAND

Brand is so much more than dressing for success. It is everything you do, every minute of the day; think of a brand as your portfolio. What does your brand say about you? What does your brand say to your organization each day? What impression do you think you are making? Are you consistent? It is the way you dress, communicate, your image, and the way you carry yourself. Your brand is your walking billboard of everything you do, communicate, project, and wear.

A brand is a way of personally marketing yourself in your career. So, before you can build your brand in person and through social media, you have to be self-aware. As you develop your career, you want to be known as a thought leader.

In the area of social media, think about where you post and what you post. What would your employer say about these posts? Would they believe you demonstrate company values? Or would they think they had made a bad decision hiring you? This is your digital fingerprint, and it follows you throughout your career.

The reality is, your posts can help or harm your career. Some prospective employees were not offered positions because of Facebook and other social media postings. Examples of such posts are Saturday night bar shots, foul language, provocative dress, etc. Whether you like it or not, nothing is off the record. Big brother really is watching. On the other hand, some prospective employees were hired because of their strong brands, posts, and contributions they made on their social-media accounts. Examples of posts include a professional photo of yourself, volunteer work such as the Food Bank, Habitat for Humanity, family outings, etc. These demonstrate strong values.

LinkedIn is the most effective business tool. Take the time to build your profile. Learn how to do this. There are books, online resources, other LinkedIn profiles, and LinkedIn University to help you. Do you have a professional photograph for your social-media accounts? Is your resume updated? How strong are your connections? How did you invite them? How many groups do you belong to? What videos, articles, or pictures are you posting/sharing? Do you have a strong headline? Do you blog or post, so you can begin to become a thought leader? Do you have strong recommendations for you on your LinkedIn profile? These recommendations on LinkedIn can enhance your career visibility opportunities. Choose wisely when asking for professional recommendations. Many years ago, I worked for an organization as President in one of the operating units. The President of the parent corporation was leaving, and I knew him well. He knew my work well. I asked him for a recommendation on LinkedIn when I was first setting up my profile. Truly I never thought about it again. Fast forward six years; I had left my company and was interviewing for a new position with a new company. I was flown to Chicago for a face-to-face interview. While I was waiting, the Human Resources recruiter came to meet me and talk with me. The first thing she said was "I checked out your LinkedIn profile." She said to me, "You have impressive recommendations." I had totally forgotten about those recommendations. The man who was going to interview me for a new position with a new company was the former President of the parent corporation I had worked for those many years ago. It is obvious this recommendation helped me to get an opportunity to interview. Oh, and yes, I did get the new job.

Beyond social media is your brand at work. How do you show up? Are you helpful? Do you consistently do your best work? Do you dress professionally every day? Do you read your emails before you hit "send" to make sure there are no typos? Do you send professional messages? No one can be an expert in everything, so ask questions. Seek out more experienced people and learn from them. Seek out thought leaders and see what they are doing. You are unique, so capitalize on your strengths.

There are so many great places to seek out how to improve your brand. In 2004, Fast Company Magazine featured the article "Brand Your Survival Kit," written by Tom Peters. To deepen your understanding, check out this article to learn how you can improve your brand. Your brand is your reputation every day.

Self-Assesment Questions

Question:
What does your brand communicate about you?

Response:

Question:
What would people say about you, if you were not in the room? If you do not know, find out.

Response:

Question:
How self-aware are you? 1 being poor and 10 being excellent

Response:

Question:
On a scale of 1-10, how strong is your brand?
- a. Face-to-face
- b. Communication
- c. Social Media accounts

Response:

Question:
What is one area in which you could improve your brand at work?

Response:

Question:
Have you set up a LinkedIn profile? How can it be improved?

Response:

Question:
What is one area in which you could improve your brand on your social-media accounts? Is there anything you have posted in the past that might have you concerned?

Response:

Question:
How will you learn more about developing your personal brand?

Response:

Question:

What is one action step you can take to improve your brand?

Response:

Question:

How will you know you are making progress?

Response:

Coach/Mentor Questions

Q: Describe your brand's self-assessment.

Response:

Q: What did you learn from the Fast Company article on "Brand Your Survival Kit" by Tom Peters?

Response:

Q: Did you ask others for feedback at work?

Response:

Q: Did you ask others for feedback on your social-media accounts?

Response:

> **Q: Did you learn anything new?**

Response:

> **Q: Did any comments surprise you?**

Response:

> **Q: After a review of your LinkedIn profile, I think I can offer some suggestions. Are you open to this type of feedback?**

Response:

> **Q: What is one action you can take to improve in this area?**

Response:

Q: How will you measure your improvement in this area?
Response:

Q: How can I support you?
Response:

KIM NUGENT

COMMUNICATION

" The art of communication is the language of leadership.
— James Humes

C IS FOR COMMUNICATION

How effective are your communication skills? People judge others within seconds, often based on speaking skills. Do you relate well to others – peers, staff members, managers, and senior management? Do you struggle with how to get your meaning across to others? Do you get nervous? Do you overshare details of your personal life at work? Depending on your communication level, check out the following organizations to enhance your confidence and communication skills: Dale Carnegie Training, Toastmasters International, and National Speakers Association (NSA) in your area. Located in major cities, Dale Carnegie is an excellent organization that specializes in public-speaking training. Toastmasters International is a great organization to join in your local area to practice your speaking skills. National Speakers Association is for professional speakers and those who speak often in their leadership positions.

What about your writing skills? Are your emails, texts, and presentations clear and appropriate for the intended receiver or audience? Have you ever created confusion by your poorly worded emails and texts? Do you read, use spell-check and resources such as Grammarly© before hitting the "send" button? If writing is a weakness, it can be improved with deliberate practice. We can all improve our communication skills no matter what role we hold within an organization. There are many significant online resources to help you improve, so check them out. You do not want to create a negative impression from behind your computer, without ever leaving your office.

What about your listening skills? Do you wait for the person to finish what they are saying before you talk or interrupt? Are you thinking about what you are going to say without paying attention to what the other person is saying? Have you learned to ask questions instead of always talking? This is a skill that must be practiced. If you do not think so, have you ever played the telephone game? It is a game of five people. You tell the first person something and they must repeat it to the next person. By the time you get to the fifth person, the original conversation is not at all the same conversation. This is how rumors start in organizations, simply because of poor listening skills and rephrasing. As your listening improves, so will all your relationships. There are personal-development classes that are offered to help you improve in this area.

While all these skills are critical to career success, most communication models suggest that 7% is verbal and 93% of our communication is non-verbal. The 93% is broken down into 55% body language and 38% tone of voice (Yaffe, 2011, p. 1).

Poor communication skills create problems at work for you and the organization. As you have reviewed A-Attitude, B-Brand, and C-Communication, how would you assess yourself? Where are your opportunities for self-improvement? You have taken the first three steps to becoming more aware of who you are and who you can become. Let's keep going!

Self-Assessment Questions

Question:

Rate your communication skills on a scale of 1-10 with 1 being poor and 10 being excellent.

Response:

_____ Listening

_____ Speaking

_____ Writing

_____ Presenting

_____ Facilitating

_____ Nonverbal Communication

_____ Body Language

_____ Tone of Voice

Question:

What is an area you need to start on first?

Response:

Question:

What is one area you could improve your communication skills at work?

Response:

Question:
What outside resources will help you improve in this area?

Response:

Question:
Have you ever participated in Toastmasters, Dale Carnegie, National Speakers Association or personal-development courses to improve your communication?

Response:

Question:
How will you know you are making progress?

Response:

Coach/Mentor Questions

Q: Describe your communication skill strengths.
Response:

Q: Describe your communication skill weaknesses.
Response:

Q: How important do you think effective communication skills are for our organization?
Response:

Q: Have you ever participated in Toastmasters, Dale Carnegie, National Speakers Association or personal-development courses to improve your communication?
Response:

Promotion Protocol

Q: Are you open to joining a local Toastmasters group?
Response:

Q: What is one action you can take to improve in this area?
Response:

Q: How will you measure your improvement in this area?
Response:

Q: How can I support you?
Response:

D

DEPTH

> " To nurture the sort of relationships that will surely help propel you towards accomplishing great things, you need to forget transactional networking and focus on having in-depth conversations with fewer people about subjects you really care about.
>
> — Naveen Jain

D IS FOR DEPTH

Do you have depth? Are you driven for a bigger purpose in life? Have you traveled to other parts of the world and apply what you learn to your life? Do you interact with all different types of people? Do you try and experience new things? Do you read, listen to podcasts, and seek more knowledge? Do you speak more than one language? Do you seek to build your character? Have you developed your creativity such as writing, painting, dancing, or playing an instrument? If not, what is the obstacle? What do you tell yourself? With whom do you surround yourself; positive people who encourage you and challenge you; or people who will bring you down and add no value?

According to Mark Myhre (2005), writer and emotional healing coach, depth is defined as a way to add richness and beauty to our lives. While you might not have ever read "depth" as being a trait in a leadership book, it is a critical trait. So how can you develop more depth? Depth can be acquired over a lifetime every day, by challenging the status quo regarding learning new things, expanding your character, and seeking purpose and meaning to life. You are looking to expand your thinking and your interests. You have a variety of interests and become more interesting as you share with others. As you do this, your energy expands, and you become more self-actualized.

Depth takes consistent action. It is not "do one thing and stop." It is not getting a degree in philosophy. It is getting in touch with what you value. It is expanding your knowledge in all areas of your life and sharing. It is fun exploring and challenging your attitude, knowledge, and skills. Depth allows you to experience new things without judgment or expectation. Depth allows you the opportunity to connect with people at a deeper level. It is not being shallow.

Be open to new opportunities. Be open to meeting new people. Be open to travel. Think about saying yes more often than you say no. Think about the reasons you give yourself when you say no. What might happen if you answered "yes" the next time? You might be surprised how much you have in common if you take the time to get to know others. Show people what you value in them.

Self-Assessment Questions

Question:
In what areas do you need to expand your personal depth?

Response:

Question:
What is an area of interest that you want to explore or deepen first?

Response:

Question:
What is one area where you could improve your creativity, or right brain?

Response:

Question:
What is one area you could improve your business knowledge, or left brain at work?

Response:

Coach/Mentor Questions

Q: Describe how you have developed your personal depth and interests at this point in yourself.

Response:

Q: What area are you excited about expanding?

Response:

Q: What area are you nervous about expanding?

Response:

Q: What area in your life have you noticed you say "no" to instead of "yes"?

Response:

Q: Where have you said "no" in your life that you might be open to answering "yes" now?

Response:

Q: Tell me more about the reason you have not tried it or what you tell yourself you cannot do?

Response:

Q: How will you measure your improvement in this area?

Response:

Q: How can I support you?

Response:

Kim Nugent

ENERGY

" And what is a man without energy? Nothing – nothing at all.
– Mark Twain

E IS FOR ENERGY

Do you possess energy where people are drawn to you, or do you bring down the group because of your lack of energy? Think about people in your life to whom you are attracted because of their energy. How do you come across?

How can you change this if your energy level is lower? Are you taking care of yourself? Do you exercise? Do you eat healthily? Do you drink enough water? Do you get enough sleep? Do you think this is important? Do you surround yourself with positive and forward-thinking people? Do you take vacations to rejuvenate? Do you carve out downtime to recapture your creativity? Do you keep yourself inspired with quotes, books, and affirmations? Do you have a hobby you are passionate about that fulfills you? Do you approach life as the glass is half empty rather than half full and think this is all there is to life? Do you feel you are resilient at work? Do you feel loved in your relationships? Do you have a spiritual practice that uplifts you? What are you passionate about in life? What is your life purpose? What are the possibilities in your life? What do you want? What goals and actions have you put in place?

Once you tap into answering these questions, your energy level will begin to improve. Think about a time when your energy was high. You could do anything and tackle anything, like being in the zone. What caused the high level of energy? What were you doing at the time that made you feel energized? Consider the possibility you were acting on things important to you.

Create a vision for your life. Set specific goals and write them down. Make them visible to you daily. Consider creating a vision board.

Start taking better care of yourself. Many jobs today exist of being behind a computer, and we become sedentary. Make a point of getting up and moving. Walk at lunch or go work out. Take the stairs instead of the elevator. Plan out meals so you can better maintain a healthy lifestyle. Drink water throughout the day. Stop drinking the sugar drinks or souped-up energy drinks; they do not help energy levels. If you start to feel your energy subsiding, breathe.

Finally, get enough sleep to tackle the next day with the energy level that serves you best. Too many people at work are sleep deprived, and this is a real problem. According to Larry Alton (2016), professional blogger and researcher, there is a relationship between sleep and worker productivity (p. 1). We all need and want more sleep but cannot always obtain a quality night's sleep. Pay attention to what works for you. Give yourself permission to go to bed earlier so you can enjoy eight hours of sleep. Make sure you turn off all electronic devices at least an hour before going to bed to reduce stimulation. Make sure you have a good mattress, a dark room, and the right room temperature for you. These should assist in giving you the energy to tackle your day ahead. If you are a person who wakes up in the middle of the night consumed by thoughts, have a journal and pen by your bed. Write the thoughts down and go back to sleep. You can train your brain to know there is a system for capturing thoughts; this can settle your mind, so you can go back to sleep. This is a more effective approach than lying in bed, thinking, not being able to sleep and then getting up in the morning more tired than when you went to bed the night before.

Build strong and loving relationships. They will energize you. Remove yourself from toxic relationships. Toxic relationships drain you of energy.

Remember, you are worth it!

Self-Assessment Questions

Question:
On a scale of 1-10 with 1 being poor and 10 being excellent, how would you rate your energy level?

Response:

Question:
What personal energy areas could be improved upon?

Response:
_____ Healthy eating
_____ Exercise daily
_____ Drinking more water
_____ Sleeping at least 8 hours a night
_____ Relationships
_____ Setting goals

Question:
What is an area of interest to start on first?

Response:

Question:

What actions will you take?

Response:

Question:

How will you know you are making progress?

Response:

Coach/Mentor Questions

Q: Describe your personal energy level at this point in your life.
Response:

Q: How can you improve your energy level based on your personal assessment?
Response:

Q: With what area will you start?
Response:
_____ Healthy eating
_____ Exercise daily
_____ Drinking more water
_____ Sleeping at least 8 hours a night
_____ Relationships
_____ Setting goals

Q: Do you feel you surround yourself with positive people who add to your life? If there is anyone who might be toxic for you, what will you do about it?
Response:

Q: What are you passionate about? What goals have you set for yourself?
Response:

Q: What do you want your life to stand for?
Response:

Q: What do you want in your life?
Response:

Q: How will you measure your improvement in this area?
Response:

Q: How can I support you?
Response:

FOCUS

> " You can do anything as long as you have the passion, the drive, the focus, and the support.
> – Sabrina Bryan

F IS FOR FOCUS

While it is sometimes difficult to focus in this fast-paced world with competing priorities, deadlines, social media, etc., it is imperative. The truth is, our attention spans are becoming shorter and shorter, but it is possible to work on improving your focus. While we all have been told that multitasking is excellent, the reality is that you can only do one thing at a time well.

When you get to the office, get ready to work. Focus on the most urgent items, then the essential projects for the day. Stop avoiding or procrastinating doing the critical tasks or problems; it only adds stress to your life. Save the less important tasks for later in the day, when your energy level might be less. You will find you are more productive and more fulfilled each day.

Make a list of things that distract you and keep them to a minimum or eliminate them. Block out time on your calendar for projects. Schedule the deadline date on the calendar and work backward to make sure you fulfill your part of the project on time. Do not schedule every minute of the day. Take short breaks every so often to reenergize.

Do not log into your social-media accounts while at work unless that is your job. They distract and eat up valuable time. If your job allows, block out time to check email only three times a day. Answer the emails, delete, or file for follow up. Deal with emails one at a time. Also, I have noticed that some people waste a lot of time talking to co-workers for long periods of time, thus wasting valuable work time. While it may seem like a good idea at the time, you pay for it in working later to get your work done to catch up. Wasting time creates more stress and anxiety because you have run out of time. If procrastinating or wasting time has become a habit, analyze the reason. Do you enjoy the adrenalin rush? Some people seem to live their lives this way without stopping to see if they can change the way they manage their lives.

So, when you begin the day, have a plan. Take stock of what you want to accomplish. List out what are time wasters. Reflect on where you need to bring more focus in your professional life and personal life. Breathe and get started.

Self-Assessment Questions

Question:
Is being focused a strength or a challenge for you?

Response:

Question:
In what areas are you distracted?

Response:

Question:
Do you think you are an adrenalin junkie?

Response:

Question:
How can you mitigate these distractions from happening? Addicted to the stress?

Response:

Question:
What is one action step you can put in place today?

Response:

Question:
How will you know you are making progress?

Response:

Coach/Mentor Questions

Q: How do you stay focused for the day?
Response:

Q: How do you stay focused for the day?
Response:

Q: What are areas of distraction for you?
Response:

Q: How can you mitigate these?
Response:

PROMOTION PROTOCOL

Q: How will you measure your improvement in this area?
Response:

Q: How can I support you?
Response:

KIM NUGENT

GRATITUDE

" Gratitude makes sense of our past, brings peace for today, and creates a vision for tomorrow.

— Melody Beattie

G IS FOR GRATITUDE

"Gratitude" is defined as being thankful. How many times each day do we miss the opportunity to be grateful? Did you know that by practicing gratitude, your life has more meaning? It changes your perspective.

Set aside time each day and start out each day by being grateful for at least three things in your life. Either say them aloud or write them down. Keeping a gratitude journal by your bed is very helpful to start and continue this practice. Putting pen to paper is a powerful tool, as it activates your brain and senses.

So many times, we fail to acknowledge the small things we are blessed to have or happen in our lives. Many people tend to focus on what is wrong. If you take the opposite approach and look for things for which to be grateful, you will find more and more blessings. As you write or state the things for which you are grateful, bring in all your senses. How does it make you feel? What do you see? What do you hear? What about a sense of touch?

So, what does expressing gratitude have to do with promotability? Everything. When you are in business, there are a series of problems to solve and that causes stress. According to Robert Emmons (2004), a world's leading gratitude expert and psychology professor at the University of California Davis, "Gratitude can be that stress buster." It allows you to generate optimism while building strength to recover more quickly from setbacks. Let people in your life know you are grateful for them. Appreciate your co-workers for their contribution.

According to Lindsay Holmes (2017), deputy editor for the Huffington Post, more gratitude equals a better life. That means a better life at home and work. If you build this habit over a 30-day period, you will feel grateful. Your whole outlook on life will be improved. Research states that expressing gratitude enhances, innovation, creativity and success. Pass it on!

Self-Assessment Questions

Question:
Do you keep a gratitude journal?

Response:

Question:
Would you be willing to write out what you are grateful for each morning?

Response:

Question:
How do you think it might change your perspective?

Response:

Question:
In what areas of your life have you taken people or situations for granted?

Response:

Question:

What is one action step you can put into place today regarding gratitude?

Response:

Question:

How will you know you are making progress?

Response:

Coach/Mentor Questions

Q: What are you grateful for at work?

Response:

Q: What are you grateful for at home?

Response:

Q: What are you grateful for from your work team?

Response:

Q: What are you grateful for in your relationships?

Response:

Q: What daily practice are you willing to take to keep gratitude at the forefront?

Response:

Q: Is there any area of your life or a person you have taken for granted?

Response:

Q: How will you measure your improvement in this area?

Response:

Q: How can I support you?

Response:

Kim Nugent

HABITS

" We are what we repeatedly do. Excellence then is not an act but a habit.

— Aristotle

H IS FOR HABITS

Do you possess good habits or bad habits? What would your friends, family, or co-workers say about your habits? You might want to interview a few trusted friends and colleagues to get an honest assessment. Often, we are blind to what we do and how it affects others.

Once again, Fast Company published an article in 2017 on bad habits to ditch. Do you possess any of these habits? Ditch These Seven Bad Habits before 2018 Starts by Gwen Moran. Read this article at https://www.fastcompany.com/40503547/ditch-these-seven-bad-habits-before-2018-starts and see if you see yourself as having possessed these habits.

Once we begin to recognize our bad habits, how can we start to change them? We all have them. You cannot change everything overnight, but you can take steps to improve one thing at a time. Describe your bad habit. What do you think is the root cause for it? If you were to change it, how would it benefit your life? With what will you replace the bad habit? What can you do instead?

Once you have identified the habit, the root cause, and with what you can replace the bad habit, next is accountability. Reach out to a co-worker or friend and have them be your accountability partner. Give yourself some time. Much has been written on this subject about how long it takes to change a habit. The time-frame ranges from 21 days to three months. It depends on the habit and the person. Commit to the time-frame. Know that you probably will make a few mistakes along the way or backslide. We are human; but do not quit. No need to justify the reasons it happened but become aware of what triggered it. Recommit yourself to making progress toward changing the habit. Tomorrow is a new day!

Realize that many habits you possess are positive. Keep them and discard what does not serve you and others. You are on the road to excellence.

Self-Assessment Questions

Question:
What habits need to change?

Response:

Question:
What is the habit you are going to work on first?

Response:

Question:
What is the underlying cause of the poor habits?

Response:

Question:
Are you willing to have an accountability partner? If so, who could be your partner?

Response:

Question:
What is the time-frame you are committing to change the habit?

Response:

Question:
How will you know you are making progress?

Response:

Question:
How will you celebrate your success?

Response:

Coach/Mentor Questions

Q: What habit have you decided to work on first?
Response:

Q: How will it lead to excellence?
Response:

Q: What is the benefit to making this change?
Response:

Q: What will it cost you if you do not make the change?
Response:

Q: How will you feel when you change this habit?
Response:

Q: Do you have an accountability partner?
Response:

Q: How will you keep this present and at the top of your mind daily?
Response:

Q: What is your time-frame?
Response:

Q: If you make a misstep, how will you recover and get back on track?
Response:

Q: How will you measure your improvement in this area?
Response:

Q: How will we celebrate your success?
Response:

Q: How can I support you?
Response:

Q: How will you feel when you change this habit?
Response:

Q: Do you have an accountability partner?
Response:

Q: How will you keep this present and at the top of your mind daily?
Response:

Q: What is your time-frame?
Response:

KIM NUGENT

INTEGRITY

> " A single lie destroys a whole reputation of integrity.
> – Baltasar Gracian

I IS FOR INTEGRITY

This is not a make-wrong word. It's doing what you say all the time regardless of whether anyone is watching you or knowing. It is integrity of self. Keeping and honoring your word. It is a state of being. It is keeping your promises to you, your friends, and family. You will be amazed how free you feel when you know you can keep your word to yourself and others, and they can count on you. It does not mean always saying yes.

Here is a situation to consider: Are you great at work about keeping your word, but when it comes to yourself not so much — or vice versa? Take a real look at your life and decide where you can improve your integrity muscle. It will take practice, but each day you make an effort, you grow. Now to make this trait real, you need to dig down deep and tell the truth to yourself.

Here are some areas to think about: Do you gossip about others? Have you taken things without paying for them? Have you taken office supplies home for personal use? Have you used the company copier for copying personal things? Do you tell little white lies and justify it? Do you exceed the speed limit? Have you ever parked in a handicapped accessible parking space, even though you are not handicapped? Do you think the rules do not apply to you? Have you hurt someone's feelings and never apologized? Have you been charged less for an item at a store and failed to tell them they charged you the wrong amount? Have you ever found money on the floor at a store and failed to turn it in? Have you disclosed confidential information about your company or a project? Have you used work time to be on social media when you were supposed to be working? Have you ever made a mistake at work and failed to own it? Did you fail to meet a company deadline? Do you follow company policies 100% of the time? Have you taken credit for someone else's work? Have you ever compromised your values? Do you have the courage to tell the truth?

Or maybe you are great at keeping your word with others but when it comes to yourself, not as much. Do you have integrity for yourself? Do you keep your word with yourself? For example, do you tell yourself you are going to go to the gym three days a week and then do not follow through?

Look to see where there are opportunities to improve each day in this area. So how can you build your integrity muscle?

Be honest. When you make a mistake, own it. Be a person of your word. Become someone everyone can count on, no matter what. Know that you can rely on yourself. Know that you are your word. The more you practice the integrity muscle, the stronger you become. It is just like working out. You know you have arrived when you can count on your word and yourself. Integrity is a crucial characteristic of leadership.

Good luck getting stronger each day!

Self-Assessment Questions

Question:
What does integrity mean to you?

Response:

Question:
Is integrity important in a leadership role?

Response:

Question:
When you read the examples, did you see yourself in any of them?

Response:

Question:

Who do you admire because of their integrity? What company displays integrity?

Response:

Question:

What examples are you aware of in business when the leader failed to have integrity? What happened? If not aware, research and share.

Response:

Question:

What is one area that you can work on for yourself?

Response:

Question:
How do you justify your behavior when your integrity is not intact?

Response:

Question:
How will you know you are making progress?

Response:

Question:
How will you know when you can keep your word? To yourself? To others?

Response:

Coach/Mentor Questions

Q: What does integrity mean to you?
Response:

Q: What did you think of some of the examples provided? Let's discuss a few.
Response:

Q: Have you ever looked at integrity in this way? What surprised you?
Response:

Q: If you were in a leadership position, how would you model it?
Response:

Q: In your current position, how do you demonstrate integrity?
Response:

Q: What happens when a leader does not model integrity? What happens to the organization? To the culture? To the people? Can you give me some specific examples?
Response:

Q: How will you measure your improvement in this area?
Response:

Q: How can I support you?
Response:

JADED

> " I suppose there are a lot of reasons to be jaded or sarcastic, but I hang onto the reasons why life is beautiful.
>
> — Kellie O'Hara

J IS FOR JADED

Are you jaded because of all the world events? Are you feeling cynical about leadership? Do you feel disappointed by athletes and people in the media? Do you think life is not fair and you have been passed over? Do you complain about those people at work? Are you the person who sits in the stands and yells but does nothing — or are you the person who sees a situation and wants to become an agent of change? Do you complain about your job, co-workers or boss? Or do you take the high road? Do you get involved in your community to improve the quality of life? Do you engage others to join you? Who are you in these scenarios? Are you in the stands or on the field?

According to the Merriam Webster dictionary, jaded is feeling "dull or cynical." Do you feel entitled to being cynical because you feel like you have been wronged at work? Do you feel like people at work are not doing their part? Did you know that being cynical is a defensive posture to try and protect yourself? But the truth is that being cynical can dramatically decrease the quality and health of your life. When you see the world from this perspective, everything is dull and there is no joy. Probably the only person suffering is you. So, if there is an opportunity for promotion at your workplace, what reason would leadership have for promoting someone who is cynical? I can't think of any, can you?

If you want to take the path to having the possibility of being promoted, you can take a different approach and begin to improve the quality of your life. You can take the high road and become an agent for change and become more positive. You can become compassionate toward others. Instead of looking for what is wrong in every situation, begin looking for what is right. Decide who you want to be. Your future is in your hands!

Self-Assessment Questions

Question:
On a scale of 1 to 10 with 1 - being feel jaded all the time and 10 being never feel jaded. How would you rate yourself?

Response:

Question:
In what areas do you struggle with cynicism?

Response:

Question:
How can you begin to change this outlook?

Response:

Question:
How will you know you are starting to shift your perspective?

Response:

Coach/Mentor Questions

Q: Are there areas at work where you feel jaded? What happened?
Response:

Q: What is the root cause?
Response:

Q: How can you change your perspective?
Response:

Q: If you have a direct report who is jaded, how would you coach that employee? How can you propose an alternative perspective?
Response:

Q: What strategies might work to improve the situation?
Response:

Q: What resources might be available?
Response:

Q: How can I support your growth in this area?
Response:

Kim Nugent

KNOWLEDGEABLE

" An investment in knowledge pays the best interest.
— Benjamin Franklin

K IS FOR KNOWLEDGEABLE

How well do you know all aspects of your role in the company? How well do you know the entire organization's operations? What do you need to know? What skills do you need that you may be lacking? Are there certifications or education that would enhance your promotability? Decide what you want to learn. Do you want to go wide or deep? Do you want to specialize in an area? Develop a plan for gaining the knowledge you need to fill in the gaps.

Knowledge is defined as facts, information, and skills you learn through education and experience. How can you increase your knowledge? You can read. You can ask questions. You can seek out a mentor/business coach. Is there training available to enhance your skill set, either inside the company or outside? Is there a professional organization you could join?

What can you volunteer to learn? You can stretch yourself and take on new projects to learn and assist others. Keep an open mind. It takes time to learn new things. You will make mistakes, but learn from them. Notice how you feel when you are learning new things. It may be uncomfortable for a while as you are outside your comfort zone.

How can you continue to enhance your technology skills? Technology may be an area where you excel but there is always more to learn; and it changes daily. You can also help others in this area if it is not their area of expertise. When the student becomes the teacher, you begin the path of mastery.

Examine other areas in your organization where you may need to learn. What is the company culture? What is the mission, vision, and values? Is the company strategic plan and goals available to you? Do you understand the financial aspects of the company you work for? Have you mastered finance in your own life? Have you read the annual report of the company if publicly traded? Do you understand it? Do you know what reports are important in your company? Can you interpret what they mean? Do you know how the metrics can be achieved? Do you participate in deliberate practice and set aside time to master a new skill? What information is missing in order for you to increase your mastery? What is the company promotion protocol? The only way to learn is to read, talk, practice, and then demonstrate mastery over time.

Self-Assessment Questions

Question:
On a scale of 1 to 10, with 1 - poorly and 10 - very well how well do you understand the following?

Response:
_____ Company culture
_____ Company mission, vision, and values
_____ Company strategic plan
_____ Company policies and procedures
_____ Company metrics
_____ Company reports
_____ Your role with this company
_____ Overall company operations
_____ Finances/Budget
_____ Technology
_____ Talent development
_____ Promotion protocol

Question:
Once you have completed the list, decide where to start. What is the first action step to increase your knowledge?

Response:

Question:
What examples are you aware of in business when the leader failed to have integrity? What happened? If not aware, research and share.

Response:

Question:
What way do you learn best?

Response:
_____ Auditory
_____ Visual
_____ Tactile-Kinesthetic
_____ Online
_____ Face-to-face
_____ Blended
_____ Research on own
_____ Books
_____ Podcasts
_____ Workshops
_____ College classes

PROMOTION PROTOCOL

Question:
What resources are available within the company to acquire new knowledge?

Response:

Question:
How can you become a highly valued contributor?

Response:

Coach/Mentor Questions

> Q: In what areas do you feel you need to gain more knowledge about company operations? Share with me your plan and list of things you need to learn so we can incorporate those into our weekly meetings.

Response:

_____ Company culture

_____ Company mission, vision, and values

_____ Company strategic plan

_____ Company policies and procedures

_____ Company metrics

_____ Company reports

_____ Your role with this company

_____ Overall company operations

_____ Finances/Budget

_____ Technology

_____ Talent development

_____ Promotion protocol

> Q: Where do you want to start? Let's create a plan.

Response:

Q: Do you have a mentor?

Response:

Q: How do you learn best?

Response:

_____ Auditory

_____ Visual

_____ Tactile-Kinesthetic

_____ Online

_____ Face-to-face

_____ Blended

_____ Research on own

_____ Books

_____ Podcasts

_____ Workshops

_____ College classes

Q: How do you want to be coached?

Response:

Q: What resources do you think you need?
Response:

Q: How can I support your growth in this area?
Response:

KIM NUGENT

LIFE-LONG LEARNER

> " Life is not about finding yourself. Life is about creating it.
> — George Bernard Shaw

L IS FOR LIFE-LONG LEARNER

Do you love to learn? Do you have a passion for trying new things? Do you engage in learning new things both inside and outside of work? Do you look for ways to stretch your creative capacity and yourself? I often feel like a kid in the candy store when it comes to learning. I feel like there is not enough time for me to learn about all the things I am interested in, but in a good and invigorating way. I make the time because it changes me. It opens my mind to new possibilities. I use what I learn from new areas to bring back to work in my role and apply it. I learn from others and broaden my perspective. I take personal-development courses to uncover my bias or understand my thinking in more effective ways.

Learning does not even have to be formal. I take every opportunity to learn something. Here are three examples. A few years ago, I had a dental emergency, and my dentist was out of town. I went to a dentist to which my sister referred me. They took care of the problem; they were highly professional. Soon they became my dentist because of how I was treated. What impressed me most was how they made notes each time you were there. I am not talking about notes about my teeth, which would be expected. Their notes were so comprehensive, and the notes included whatever we talked about whether that was family or job or travel. It was like we picked up the conversation where it left off six months prior. I think it is brilliant. Wouldn't it be great if every customer-service operation did the same thing?

The second example is my website provider. Their customer service is spectacular. No one is happy when they call for tech support because it means they are having a problem. The tech staff is patient; knowledgeable, and has always resolved my issues 100% of the time. I share these two examples as I am looking for excellent customer-service experiences all the time so I can bring it back to my operation and see how we can improve what we are doing. Where are you looking to learn?

The third example is my hairdresser. It is not a high-end salon, but every client is treated as a VIP. Every client is greeted when they walk through the door. They are called by name. The stylist works around the client's schedule, not the other way around. They strive to be on time. They offer refreshments. They ask questions to make sure they deliver the end result. They take nothing for granted. They set up the next appointment before the client leaves. Can you imagine how each client feels when they leave the salon?

If you like reading, there is an excellent resource by John R. Dijulius, III (2003) a book titled: *Secret Service: Hidden Systems That Produce Unforgettable Customer Service*. These books show you a variety of companies and the systems they use to offer exceptional customer service. As I mentioned before, you can learn a lot by studying companies outside your industry.

Do you enjoy listening to webinars or podcasts? I love TedTalks on YouTube. If you are not familiar with TED, check it out. TED stands for technology, entertainment, and design. These are 18-minute video talks by thought leaders who present high-quality information on trending topics. Check out Ted on topics that interest you and can help you in your career.

Do you belong to professional associations or organizations? Are you learning a new language, or do you spend three to four hours a day on social media thinking you are learning new things to enhance your career and promotion possibilities? Expand yourself. Do something different. Make a point of learning something new every day.

Self-Assessment Questions

Question:
On a scale of 1 to 10 rate yourself with 1 - being I do not care to learn and 10 - I have a passion for learning.

Response:
_____ Love of learning

Question:
What types of topics interest you?

Response:

Question:
What was the last personal-development course you took?

Response:

Question:
Have you watched TedTalks on YouTube? What are three of your favorites?

Response:

Question:
What was the last book you read or listened to?

Response:

Question:
What podcasts do you listen to?

Response:

Question:
Do you speak more than one language?

Response:

Question:
What interests you?

Response:

Question:
Where can lessons be learned from other industries?

Response:

Question:
What customer-service examples can you provide?

Response:

Question:
How can you encourage others to be life-long learners?

Response:

Coach/Mentor Questions

Q: How did you rate yourself on the topic of being a life-long learner? Explain.

Response:

Q: What areas of learning do you enjoy?

Response:

Q: What was the last personal development course you took?

Response:

Q: What was the last book you read or listened to?

Response:

Q: Do you watch TedTalks? If yes, what is one of your favorites?

Response:

Q: What podcasts do you listen to?
Response:

Q: Do you speak more than one language?
Response:

Q: What have you done to develop your creativity?
Response:

Q: What areas do you find less appealing?
Response:

Q: How can you encourage others to be life-long learners?
Response:

Q: Give me two examples of excellent customer service you have noticed.
Response:

Q: Give me one example of poor customer service you received.
Response:

Q: How can we share opportunities for growth in this area?
Response:

KIM NUGENT

MINDSET

> " Innovation requires an experimental mindset.
> — Denise Morrison

M IS FOR MINDSET

Do you have a fixed mindset – or a growth mindset? How do you know? When you make a mistake, do you think you should stop or quit because you failed? Do you avoid risk and challenges? What do you tell yourself? When you are learning something new, and it is challenging, and does not come quickly, what is your self-talk? Do you say to yourself, "It is something new to learn?" Do you want to be praised for the effort or the journey?

Mindset is defined as a set of attitudes one possesses. One of the best resources on the subject of mindset is Carol Dweck's book on *Mindset: The New Psychology of Success: How We can Fulfill our Potential*. Read it and see how you can develop a growth mindset in all areas of your life. Dr. Carol Dweck describes a fixed mindset as static, avoids challenges, see the effort as fruitless, ignores useful negative feedback, and feels threatened by the success of others. She then describes characteristics of a growth mindset. They are: a desire to learn, embraces challenges, is persistent, learns from criticism, and is inspired by others. Who are you?

I tested Carol Dweck's mindset theory for many years when I facilitated a graduate new-student orientation workshop each session. We had a lot of interactive activities, so the students could get the feel about what they were about to undertake in obtaining a master's degree. About midway through the orientation, I gave the graduate students an assignment. I told them at our University every student was expected to use American Psychological Association (APA) formatting in referencing all sources for their papers. I handed out a research paper to each student and had them try and find the APA errors. This was a tough assignment because they had not even started their classes. I watched with intrigue how they approached the task. Most took the paper and tried to figure something out. A few took the paper and threw it to the side in total frustration. I did not let the exercise go more than two minutes for fear of them leaving before they started. I then conducted a debrief. I asked them how they felt when I handed out the assignment. Some said they were scared, some were open to trying and some said they felt like quitting. I told them to realize they were in graduate school to learn new things. I told them I did not really expect them to be able to do the assignment. I asked them to remember the feeling they had when we did this throughout their graduate-school journey.

I wanted to begin to create a growth mindset for every person in the workshop. If they already knew how to do these things they would not need graduate school. It is a place to learn, to be challenged, and make mistakes. I then handed out an APA guide to help them do the assignment. We then went through the paper, and I pointed out the APA errors.

As I explained the difference and my intention, the students relaxed. They said it was a lesson they would never forget.

Let's take this to the business setting and your career. What is your mindset? I often heard colleagues say "This place is political." I would hear people say. "My boss is pressuring me to do…" I have heard people say, "You cannot get ahead here because I am…." I know I have never said those things as I do not see the world that way. It is not my mindset or my self-talk. I am sure there are workplaces where this exists, but is really that way or is it a fixed mindset to justify your situation and make them wrong? Truly you are the only person who knows. As you are reading this, you make take issue with me, but a coach challenges your thinking.

Self-Assessment Questions

Question:
Overall, do you feel like you have a growth mindset or a fixed mindset?

Response:

Question:
In what areas of your life, do you have a growth mindset?

Response:

Question:
In what areas of your life do you have a fixed mindset?

Response:

Question:
Do you like to be rewarded for the outcome or the journey?

Response:

Question:

What do you say to yourself when things are hard, or you are learning something for the very first time?

Response:

Question:

How can you begin to shift your mindset to a growth mindset?

Response:

Question:

How will you know you are starting to shift your perspective?

Response:

Coach/Mentor Questions

Q: Describe what you think is a growth mindset.
Response:

Q: Describe what you think is a fixed mindset.
Response:

Q: Do you feel like you have a growth mindset or fixed mindset?
Response:

Q: In what areas of your life, do you have a growth mindset?
Response:

Q: In what areas of your life do you have a fixed mindset?

Response:

Q: Do you like to be rewarded for the outcome or the journey? Explain.

Response:

Q: What do you say to yourself when things are hard, or you are learning something for the very first time?

Response:

Q: How can you begin to shift your mindset of a growth mindset?

Response:

Q: How will you know you are starting to shift your perspective?
Response:

Q: How can I encourage your growth in this area?
Response:

Q: We are halfway through the 26 traits, what you do feel you have learned to date?
Response:

Q: How do you feel you have changed?
Response:

Promotion Protocol

Kim Nugent

NETWORK

> " One of the most powerful networking practices is to provide immediate value to a new connection. This means the moment you identify a way to help someone you take action.
> — Lewis Howes

N IS FOR NETWORK

What is networking? Networking is where you develop business relationships, share information, and assist each other. What is important about building a network? Building a strong professional network is part of your career strategy. People in your network can give you advice. Determine what your target audience is. Not all events are going to be right for you. Be selective in your choices. Choose wisely when adding connections through LinkedIn, which is distinct from Facebook or other social-media choices. Stay in touch with your LinkedIn network colleagues to maintain an active network without an agenda. LinkedIn makes it very easy to stay in touch. I like to think of social media this way: LinkedIn is for business, Facebook for friends, Twitter for purpose and YouTube for subscribers.

How do I actually network? When going to a networking event, have a goal to meet one or two people. Really get to know them well. Seek out new people. Take business cards with you. I am often surprised how many people say they forgot to bring their cards. Ask them questions. Provide value; not what you want.

This is not speed dating. Ask for their business card. Repeat their name. Make a note on the back of the card when and where you met them. Follow-up within 24 hours with an email, so they have a memory of you. Do not wait to do this. The goal is not to collect business cards; it is to connect. Over time you will build strong, trusting relationships. Create a win-win relationship. The more often you do this, the more confident you become.

Your network is the golden ticket to career success only if you stay in touch and build strong relationships. Look for opportunities to connect and help people in your network instead of making it all about you. Check in with them periodically to see how they are doing and see what they might need and how you might help. You will feel great when you get to help others in your network. They, one day, might be willing to help you or mentor you.

Inc. Magazine contained an excellent article on networking called Eight Things Power Networkers Do to Make Connections by Minda Zetlin. Check it out at https://www.inc.com/minda-zetlin/8-things-power-networkers-do-make-connections.html

Self-Assessment Questions

Question:
What is the purpose of networking?

Response:

Question:
How can it help your career?

Response:

Question:
Do you enjoy networking?

Response:

Question:
In what areas of networking do you feel you need assistance?

Response:

Question:
In what areas of networking do you excel?

Response:

Question:
What was the last networking event you attended?

Response:

Question:
When and where is the next networking event you will attend?

Response:

Question:
What value can you create when networking?

Response:

Coach/Mentor Questions

Q: What networking events have you attended within our company and externally?

Response:

Q: Describe how you feel when you go to a networking event?

Response:

Q: Do you typically go alone to these events or do you bring another colleague with you?

Response:

Q: In what areas of networking do you feel you excel?

Response:

Q: In what areas of networking do you need assistance with now?
Response:

Q: Is there a networking event that you are interested in attending but have not done so yet?
Response:

Q: What is stopping you?
Response:

Q: How can I support your growth in this area?
Response:

Kim Nugent

OPPORTUNITY

" Success is where preparation and opportunity meet.
— Bobby Unser

O IS FOR OPPORTUNITY

Be observant. Look for opportunities to contribute and make a difference. When problems get presented, think through how you can find ways to bring value instead of complaining.

One of the best examples of this happened to me when I first started my career in higher education as a new faculty member. I had been teaching at this school for three months before the fall session. The department director told me my class in the fall session started at 7 a.m. So the first day of class, I arrived early, set up my class and by 7:10 a.m. no students were in class. I thought it was strange, so I headed to the Registrar's office to see the actual class schedule. The schedule said my class started at 9 a.m., not 7 a.m. I decided to just wait in the faculty/staff lounge until class was to begin. Honestly it was the best two hours I ever spent. As each new faculty member came into the lounge, they would ask me where to turn in attendance sheets, how to use the copy machine, where were the mailboxes, the class schedule, Registrar's office, etc.? I helped each and every person even though I was new myself and did not know everything.

I went to teach my class at 9 a.m. The class ended at noon. I promptly went to the Dean of Education's office and asked to speak with him. I had only met him one time and I was nervous. His personal assistant said he had time to see me. I explained what had occurred to me that morning, which was that a lot of new teachers were not sure what to do on the first day of class. I told him in my previous role in the hospitality industry we always held a new employee orientation before anyone started. It helped them feel better connected and more confident in the role. He said, "Great idea. You should do that." I laughed to myself, as I had not been given an orientation but I said "Yes, I would be happy to do this." I knew I needed to partner with someone at the school who knew the building, the programs, and all the floors. I found that person in Cliff Willson. I asked him if he would help and he said yes. So, for the next two years each quarter, we held the new-employee orientation. Each time we delivered the orientation, it became better and better.

I could have complained about the situation, but I chose a different approach. I believe that because of this situation, it propelled me into having some of the most amazing opportunities in higher education over the next 17 years.

So, think about problems you see in your organization. Reframe problems as opportunities and see where your career takes you.

Self-Assessment Questions

Question:

What problems or gaps have you noticed in the organization that could be viewed as opportunities?

Response:

Question:

When have you taken the initiative to bring solutions to your organization? Provide three examples.

Response:
1.
2.
3.

Question:

What kind of impact do you want to make?

Response:

Question:

How will you know you are making progress?

Response:

Coach/Mentor Questions

> Q: Did you learn anything new when you read the example shared as an opportunity?

Response:

> Q: What problems or gaps have you noticed in the organization that could be viewed as opportunities?

Response:

> Q: When have you taken the initiative to bring solutions to your organization? Provide three examples.

Response:
 1.
 2.
 3.

> Q: What kind of impact do you want to make?

Response:

Q: What is one action you can take to improve in this area?

Response:

Q: How will you measure your improvement in this area?

Response:

Q: How can I support you?

Response:

Kim Nugent

PROBLEM-SOLVER

> " Never bring the problem-solving stage into the decision-making stage. Otherwise, you surrender yourself to the problem rather than the solution.
> — Robert Schuller

P IS FOR PROBLEM-SOLVER

Being known as a great problem solver is a career enhancer. Organizations value employees, managers, and leaders who can solve problems. Since business and technology are moving at such a rapid pace, we must be able to solve problems to grow and develop; both professionally and for the organization.

While many an employee may find ways to solve problems through trial and error, there are many other significant problem-solving models to consider. One of my favorite books on the subject was written by Thomas Connellan, PhD. The title of the book is *Bringing Out the Best in Others!: 3 Keys for Business Leaders, Educators, Coaches, and Parents*. This is a must-read book for everyone.

My personal experience having used and taught the model is that if you use the three keys together, you really can improve performance 10 to 20%. Improvements can be made at work, on your team, and in your family. There is value in every aspect of your life by reading and applying these three keys: positive expectations, accountability/responsibility, and feedback.

Dr. Connellan gives specific examples you can apply it to your life. There are so many great and simple tips to bring about positive changes. Dr. Connellan helps reframe the way you provide feedback to produce a better result without putting people on the defensive. He ends the book by sharing a real problem-solving model. As with any new skill, it must be practiced.

MindTools has excellent articles for career professionals. Henry Kaiser wrote one such article on "What is Problem Solving?" As Mr. Kaiser is quoted as saying, "Problems are only opportunities in work clothes." Check out the whole story at https://www.mind-tools.com/pages/article/newTMC_00.htm

Self-Assessment Questions

Question:
When problems are presented, how do you begin to solve them?

Response:

Question:
Research 3 problem-solving models to help you become a better problem solver.

Response:
1.
2.
3.

Question:
What problems have you solved at work? Provide three examples.

Response:

Question:
How will you know you are making progress in the area of problem-solving?

Response:

Coach/Mentor Questions

Q: When problems are presented, how do you begin to solve them?

Response:

Q: When have you taken the initiative to bring solutions to your organization? Provide three examples.

Response:
1.
2.
3.

Q: What problems have you solved at work? Provide three examples.

Response:
1.
2.
3.

Q: When you begin to solve a problem, do you look at the root cause?

Response:

Q: How do you identify the issue? How do you determine the solution(s)?

Response:

Q: How can you help your team members become better problem solvers?

Response:

Q: How will you know you are making progress in the area of problem-solving?

Response:

Q: How can I support you?

Response:

Kim Nugent

QUESTION

" *The art and science of asking questions is the source of all knowledge.*

— Thomas Berger

Q IS FOR QUESTION

The art of asking questions seems to be dwindling due to the fast pace of business. Taking the time to ask questions will save you time and give you the information you need to make informed decisions. Ask questions. Questions provide answers. They inform. Questions are information disguised as power. The more you ask, the more you learn about people, processes, plans, and passion. The more questions you ask, the more interesting you become. It is not in what you know, it is what you learn. If this is an area of weakness for you, learn how to ask essential questions.

There are specific types of questions for particular situations. As far back as Socrates (470-339 BC), the art of asking and answering questions was used to stimulate critical thinking. It helps inform and educate.

Organizations like the Foundation for Critical Thinking serve to promote asking questions and providing resources to educators, healthcare practitioners and the military since the 1980s.

In the education industry, teachers use Blooms Taxonomy to provide questions to engage and stimulate discussions. Dr. Benjamin Bloom created the six levels of questioning in 1956. They were: knowledge, comprehension, application, analysis, synthesis, and evaluation. Anderson and Krathwohl, students of Dr. Bloom, updated Bloom's Taxonomy in 2001. The updated version is stated in terms of verbs instead of nouns to denote questioning as an action and is not static. They are: remember, understand, apply, analyze, evaluate, and create. There is also a digital version of the taxonomy to meet the needs of today's digital audience.

Even the Dale Carnegie organization believes that asking questions is an essential people skill. Check out their books and videos online. It helps inform and build connections with others. What questioning models does your organization use?

Reduce your talking, ask more questions, and increase your listening capacity. It might keep you from jumping to the wrong conclusions. If you are not listening, you are filling in the blanks with your own thoughts or meaning, which can distort the outcome of the communication.

It might surprise you how attractive you become to others when you are fully present and listen. Think about it. How do you feel when someone really listens to you?

Self-Assessment Questions

Question:
How is problem-solving related to asking questions?

Response:

Question:
Have you ever thought about the types of questions you ask?

Response:

Question:
Does your organization have a questioning model they use?

Response:

Question:

Research three questioning resources. It can be online, book, podcast or TedTalk. Be ready to discuss.

Response:
1.
2.
3.

Question:

How will you know you are improving your questioning ability?

Response:

Coach/Mentor Questions

Q: It seems that problem-solving and asking questions are related. Explain to me the relationship and how it can enhance your promotability traits.

Response:

Q: What is critical thinking?

Response:

Q: Tell me in your own words how asking questions supports critical thinking?

Response:

Q: Have you ever analyzed the type of questions you ask?

Response:

Q: What did you find when you researched three questioning resources? Let's discuss.

Response:

Q: How will you know you are improving your questioning ability?

Response:

Q: How can you help your team members become better at asking questions rather than jumping to conclusions or voicing their opinions?

Response:

Q: Compare and contrast two people on your team and their critical thinking ability.

Response:

Q: Create a plan for continuing to develop your critical thinking skills.

Response:

Q: How can I support you in the area of questioning?

Response:

KIM NUGENT

RESPONSIBILITY

" You cannot escape the
responsibility of tomorrow
by evading it today.
— Abraham Lincoln

R IS FOR RESPONSIBILITY

So, who are you in the area of responsibility? Are you naturally responsible at work, for your family, for your community? Or do you shy away from responsibility because it seems hard or demanding?

Responsibility is defined as being accountable; taking action on your own, or taking the opportunity to act independently. Being responsible is one way to stand out in front of your boss, so you get noticed. What are the actual steps to taking on more responsibility? Alex Cavoulous, President and Founder of The Muse, wrote an excellent article titled "5 Ways to Take on More Responsibility at Work". First, let's assume you are good at your current role at work.

In your next coaching meeting, talk with your boss about the knowledge and skills you want to develop further. Look for opportunities to help team members. Decide what areas in which you want to become an expert — the person everyone in the company goes to because you stay on top of developments and trends.

Alex Cavoulus suggests setting up a Google alert for topics relevant to your industry (p. 3). You get daily email updates this way. I have done this myself and find it a huge time-saver.

One of the traits I look for in developing high-potential employees is the one who takes the initiative; the employee that brings me new ideas or solutions. Someone who is proactive rather than waiting to be told what to do next. For me, that employee waits to be told what to do is marginal. In this fast-paced world, we cannot accept marginal or just doing your job. Demonstrate your leadership skills inside and outside the office. You do not need a title to demonstrate you have what it takes to become an exceptional leader.

Are you the person at work who blames others, finds fault with managers, your situation, the economy, and/or society? Do you blame others for you not getting the promotion? Are you playing the victim, or are you taking personal responsibility for having a good job, good relationships, and good life? Who are you in this responsibility scenario?

Ron Haskins wrote an article for Brookings Institute called the "Sequence of Personal Responsibility." Check out this article at https://www.brookings.edu/articles/the-sequence-of-personal-responsibility/

Self-Assessment Questions

Question:
What does the responsibility quote mean to you?

Response:

Question:
Be prepared to talk to your boss at your next coaching meeting.

Response:

Question:
What additional project would you like to take on and discuss with your boss?

Response:

Question:
What skills and knowledge do you want to develop next?

Response:

Question:

Do you see opportunities to help a team member who may be overworked? What are they? Be ready to discuss.

Response:

Question:

In what area do you want to become an expert?

Response:

Question:

Taking the initiative is critical to the promotion pathway. If you took a self-assessment, would you consider yourself average or a high-potential employee? What initiative have you taken or could seek to change the situation?

Response:

Coach/Mentor Questions

Q: *You cannot escape the responsibility of tomorrow by evading it today.* — Abraham Lincoln. What does this quote mean to you?

Response:

Q: Let's discuss you taking on more responsibility at work. What additional project would you like to take on?

Response:

Q: What skills and knowledge do you want to develop next?

Response:

Q: What do you think senior managers value in high-potential employees?

Response:

Q: Do you see opportunities to help a team member who may be overworked?

Response:

Q: In what area do you want to become an expert?

Response:

Q: Have you set up a daily Google© alert to get started? On what topic(s)?

Response:

Q: How can you develop taking the initiative?

Response:

Q: How can I support you in the area of responsibility?

Response:

Promotion Protocol

Kim Nugent

SELF-AWARENESS

> " Knowing yourself is key to all wisdom.
>
> – Aristotle

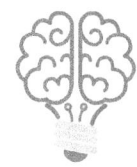

S IS FOR SELF-AWARENESS

Self-awareness is key to your success. If you know yourself, you get it. Have you looked in the mirror lately? How self-aware are you? Do you know where your blind spots are? Can you identify your strengths? Do you know your weaknesses? If you want to improve your self-awareness, here are some approaches.

You might want to consider conducting your own personal 360 assessment. Ask three to six people, (who you trust and will give honest feedback, but who are not friends who will just tell you what you want to hear) the following: name three of your strength areas, two areas that need to be developed, one thing they find frustrating about you, what they wish for you, what is an area of expertise for you, what are your blind spots and how you can improve and challenge yourself. You will be amazed at what you learn about yourself.

There are company 360 performance assessments that can help. Does your company have these for high-potential employees? Have you taken any online self-awareness assessments such as

Myers-Briggs™, DISC™, StrengthsFinder™, Enneagram™, emotional intelligence, learning styles, career and leadership assessments? What did you learn?

I recently asked a few professional friends what they think their managers think of them, such as, how do you think your managers think you present yourself at work? How would they describe your traits such as style? Tone? Nonverbal expressions? Time-management ability? Team player? Problem-Solver? Respectful? Contributor? Communication style, personality, etc.?

They said they had no idea. Not knowing is a huge problem. If you do not know what management is thinking, how will you ever get promoted?

Self-Assessment Questions

Question:
Based on the interviews you conducted what did you learn?

Response:

Question:
What are three of your strength areas?

Response:

Question:
What are two areas that need to be developed?

Response:

Question:
What is one thing they find frustrating about you?

Response:

Question:
What do they wish for you?

Response:

Question:
What is an area of expertise for you?

Response:

Question:
What are your blind spots?

Response:

Question:
How can you improve and challenge yourself?

Response:

Coach/Mentor Questions

Q: Based on the interviews you conducted what did you learn?

Response:

Q: Based on the interviews you conducted what surprised you?

Response:

Q: Have you taken any online self-awareness assessments? If yes, what did you learn or confirm?

Response:

Q: Have you ever taken any personal-development courses to discover your blind spots? If so, what courses? What did you find out?

Response:

> Q: To be considered a high-potential candidate, what traits are essential to leadership or promotability?

Response:

> Q: How can I support you in your quest for self-assessment?

Response:

KIM NUGENT

THANK YOU

" Make it a habit of telling people thank you. To express your appreciation, sincerely and without the expectation of anything in return. Truly appreciate those around you, and you'll soon find many others around you. Truly appreciate life, and honestly you will find you have more of it.

— Ralph Marston

T IS FOR THANK YOU

When was the last time you said, "Thank you"? Those two words are some of the most important words for your career and your life. When was the last time you wrote a handwritten "thank you" note? Not an email or a tweet but a real handwritten note. You might think this is old school, but the impression you make by doing this speaks volumes. You taking the time to acknowledge someone means a great deal.

Think about opportunities to say thank you. Did your mentor give you some solid advice? Did you seek a job recommendation? Did someone help you with a letter of recommendation? Did you go out on a job interview and did you write a follow-up thank you? Were you given a job, and did you say thank you? Were you given a promotion, and did you say thank you? Did you thank your team members when they completed a project on time? Were you given a bonus, and did you say thank you? You might be thinking, "Hey I earned it…what's the big deal"? That attitude is an entitlement attitude. How about being grateful and saying thank you instead?

Did a co-worker take the time to help you out? Did someone remember your birthday or work anniversary? Did someone take you to coffee, lunch, or dinner and they paid? My husband often takes me to coffee. He knows I love it. I say thank you every time. I appreciate him and the gesture. I am not saying thank you in order to get him to do it again. I appreciate it every time. It makes me feel good, and I know he feels appreciated.

Did you attend a company dinner or event? Did you thank the host? Did you say thank you? Did someone drive you to a meeting? Did you say thank you? When was the last time you thanked your boss?

As you can see from the above examples, there are ample opportunities to say thank you. If this is not your strong suit, schedule a reminder on your calendar to do this weekly at a minimum. Try it and see what happens! Make this a habit each week.

Self-Assessment Questions

Question:
Where have you noticed opportunities to say thank you?

Response:

Question:
Have you noticed missed opportunities to say thank you?

Response:

Question:
How does it make you feel when you say or write a thank you note?

Response:

Question:
Does this come naturally?

Response:

Question:

Do you need to schedule a reminder on your calendar?

Response:

Question:

How important in business do you think it is to say thank you?

Response:

Coach/Mentor Questions

Q: There is a statement that is often quoted that "employees do not quit organizations, they quit people." What does this mean to you?

Response:

Q: What kind of employee or leader do you want to be?

Response:

Q: How important is it that employees and team members feel appreciated?

Response:

Q: What makes you feel appreciated at work?

Response:

Q: Where have you noticed opportunities to say thank you?
Response:

Q: Have you noticed missed opportunities to say thank you?
Response:

Q: How important in business do you think it is to say thank you?
Response:

Q: How can I further support you in developing your "thank-you" muscle?
Response:

Promotion Protocol

KIM NUGENT

UNIQUE

" A human being is a single being. Unique and unrepeatable.
— Eileen Caddy

U IS FOR UNIQUE

You are unique and talented, so try not to compare yourself to others. This is true at work, at play, and in life. I enjoy taking yoga classes. I love the way it makes me feel. The teachers are always reminding us not to compare our practice to others.

Every person comes to yoga each day. Some days the postures are natural. Some days the poses are more challenging. Regardless, I am mindful of my self-talk. It is always positive. I made a point of going to yoga and giving myself the gift of an hour. I do not look around and compare myself to new practitioners or experienced practitioners. I see the beauty in each person. After all, it is my practice.

I believe this is also true at work; your uniqueness can be fully expressed through your authenticity. You are real, genuine, and one-of-a-kind. Positively capitalize on your uniqueness. Be engaging, fresh, current, and relevant. Being unique is not being or feeling superior. The Yoga One studio owner, Roger Rippy, and author of the *Love Revolution*, shared his very own story about this when he grew up. He said, "You have to run your own race." He added, "The question is how you acknowledge, appreciate, develop what your uniqueness is, and what you have."

Where are you exceptional?
What do you love doing?
What do you enjoy?
How can you serve others?
What inspires you?

Be willing to share information and help others no matter what age. Reinforce the idea that the company made a good decision to hire you.

Self-Assessment Questions

Question:
Where are you exceptional?

Response:

Question:
What do you love doing?

Response:

Question:
What do you enjoy?

Response:

Question:
How can you serve others?

Response:

Question:
What inspires you?

Response:

Coach/Mentor Questions

Q: Each and every person is unique. Where are you exceptional? How does that serve you?

Response:

Q: What do you love doing?

Response:

Q: Who does it serve?

Response:

Q: How can you share this with others?

Response:

Q: What do you enjoy? How can you share with others to better serve them?

Response:

Q: What inspires you? How can you use your inspiration to serve others?

Response:

Q: What have you always wanted to do? How can that serve others?

Response:

KIM NUGENT

VISION

" The visionary starts with
a clean sheet of paper
and reimagines the world.
— Malcolm Gladwell

V IS FOR VISION

What vision do you have for your life? Visualize what you want for yourself. What do you love doing? What type of career? What job roles? What salary do you want to earn? What do you want for financial security? What educational level do you want to attain? Where do you want to live? What do you want your relationships to look like? What hobbies do you enjoy? What about spirituality?

Who do you see yourself becoming? How does it feel? What do you see? Make a mental picture. Write it down. Create a vision board that inspires you, motivates, brings you joy. Place it where you see it every day. There is scientific evidence to support the power of visualization. What you focus on, you achieve.

What are people saying about you? The more you can bring all your senses into this vision you have for yourself, the more likely you will achieve it. Write it down. Look at it every day. Repeat it as an affirmation. Write down the goals you want to achieve. Do you believe it is possible? Great, if yes. Get yourself out of the way and make it happen. You are more likely to achieve the life you want, if you write your goals down, and revisit them daily.

As an emerging leader, it is imperative that you have a vision of where you want to take the organization, department, or team. The more that you can paint the picture for them, the more likely you will achieve it. When you are storytelling about the vision, bring in all senses.

One of my former bosses asked us to engage in this great exercise. He would describe the project we were working on in detail. He would then ask us to close our eyes and think about three years from now. He would say "Let's pretend we are at a company picnic celebrating our success. What would we have accomplished? What were people saying about the organization internally and externally? How did you feel? What was the day like? What sounds could you hear? What did you see around you?" By the time we finished the exercise, everyone could see in their own mind's eye where we were going and how we would feel when we got there. It is truly inspiring! At subsequent meetings, he would remind us the picture of the picnic, so we would not lose sight of where we were going and what we could accomplish.

Good luck!

Self-Assessment Questions

Question:
What do you want for yourself and your life?

Response:

Question:
What type of career? What job roles? What salary do you want to earn?

Response:

Question:
What do you want for financial security?

Response:

Question:
What educational level do you want to attain?

Response:

Question:
Where do you want to live?

Response:

Question:
What do you want your relationships to look like?

Response:

Question:
What hobbies do you enjoy?

Response:

Question:
What about spirituality?

Response:

Coach/Mentor Questions

Q: As an emerging leader, it is imperative that you have a vision of where you want to take the organization, or department or team. How would you describe the picture?

Response:

Q: What is the story?

Response:

Q: If you were the leader, could you lead the picnic exercise as described? How would you bring in all the senses? Share your version of this exercise with me.

Response:

KIM NUGENT

WHITE LIES

❝ White lies always introduce
others of a darker complexion.
— William S. Paley

WHITE LIES

I am often surprised at how people tell white lies. They feel justified for whatever reason. Example: "I am going to take home office supplies. It is no big deal. The company can afford it." Would you feel the same way if you owned the company?

Years ago, I took over a company that was in desperate financial trouble. I was uncertain for a time whether we would meet payroll every other week. I needed the employees to understand the situation without causing panic. So, I had a little fun with it, and I asked them to all return our special signature pens the next day. I called it "Amnesty Day." I was looking for a thousand ways to reduce expenses while not losing sight of all the details. The next day we had over 1,000 custom signature pens returned. Have I made my point?

For the employees, it seemed like no big deal, but it was indeed a symbol for all of us to work together and turn the situation around, and we did. You might feel someone mistreated you, you deserve something and you justify it. The truth is that white lies become bigger lies. Over time, people forget what the truth is. Lying has a way of holding you hostage. You can justify all you want, but it costs you. It costs you integrity, relationships, jobs, freedom, and authenticity.

A second example is when you tell your supervisor the report is done but it isn't. You built in time to turn it in on time but you actually lied to your boss about present state of the report.

Another third example is in social media. How truthful do you think you are in the way you present yourself in social media? Your photo? Your resume? Your relationships? Your reputation? Is it the truth or a lie? Be careful: big brother, and your employer are always watching.

Self-Assessment Questions

Question:
Where have you told white lies?

Response:

Question:
How did you justify it?

Response:

Question:
What did it cost you? Or what could it cost you?

Response:

Question:
Do you ever think white lies become more significant over time?

Response:

Coach/Mentor Questions

Q: What did you think about "Amnesty Day" and the returned pens?

Response:

Q: Do you think most people feel justified in telling white lies? What do you think the point of it is?

Response:

Q: Do you think there is ever a time when a white lie is justified?

Response:

Q: As a future leader, how can you create a culture of truth and integrity?

Response:

Q: How do you model transparency?

Response:

Q: How can I support you?

Response:

Kim Nugent

X-FACTOR FOR LIFE

> " The X-Factor saved me.
> — James Arthur

X IS FOR X-FACTOR

I believe exceptional leaders have the X-Factor. These traits for exceptional leaders are distinct from general leadership traits. I think most people cannot describe the traits of an exceptional leader, as they have not had the experience of working for one. Based on my experience, I created these traits that exist in exceptional leaders as follows:

- Authentic: Genuine, real, transparent, and comfortable with who they are
- Depth: Understand the organization across all boundaries and themselves; willing to try new things; take risks
- Eclectic: Come to the position with a varied background of experiences; unique
- Energy of Being: Energy level has what it takes in good times and bad; resilient
- Generosity of Spirit: The ability to connect and relate to human beings; heart-centered; culturally sensitive
- Texture: Brings a sense of creativity when approaching each situation; multi-dimensional
- Visionary: Able to plan for the future and inspire others to achieve the vision, mission, and goals

So, what is your X-Factor? What is your unique talent? How can you positively impact the outcome of the organization in your role?

Can you relate to any of the exceptional leadership traits? Are you authentic? Creative? Eclectic? Have depth? Do you have a variety of experiences? Do you have a presence? Do you have texture? Do you have credibility? Are you innovative? Do you have a generosity of spirit? Are you interesting? Are you visionary? How many of these talents do you possess? Given your assessment, would you want to promote yourself? Tell the truth.

Self-Assessment Questions

Question:
What is your X-Factor?

Response:

Question:
What is your unique talent?

Response:

Question:
How can you positively impact the outcome of the organization in your role?

Response:

Question:
Can you relate to any of the seven exceptional leadership traits?

Response:
a. Authentic
b. Depth
c. Eclectic
d. Energy of Being
e. Generosity of Spirit
f. Texture
g. Visionary

Question:
How many of these talents do you possess?

Response:

Question:
Given your assessment, would you want to promote you?

Response:

Coach/Mentor Questions

Q: Let's discuss each of these seven traits of an exceptional leader. What does it mean to be Authentic?

Response:

Q: What does it mean to have Depth?

Response:

Q: What does it mean to be Eclectic? What experiences do you bring?

Response:

Q: What is your Energy level? How resilient are you in bad times? Give me an example.

Response:

Q: Do you feel you have a Generosity of Spirit? Do you think you have the ability to connect and relate to human beings?

Response:

Q: Do you have Texture? Do you have the ability to bring a sense of creativity when approaching each situation? Give me an example.

Response:

Q: Do you feel that one day you have the ability to be Visionary? Do you think you have the ability to inspire others to achieve the vision, mission, and goals? Give me an example.

Response:

Q: How can I support you?

Response:

KIM NUGENT

YEARNING

" There are three ingredients for a good life: learning, earning, and yearning.
— Christopher Morley

Y IS FOR YEARNING

Do you have an innate yearning to become a better you? Do you have a zest for life? Do you have a love for learning? Do you yearn to earn? Do you yearn to travel and experience new things? This is not to say you are not satisfied but rather have an energy that encompasses the essence of your being. Yearning is not related to age. Yearning can exist any age.

Yearning is defined as a strong desire to….
I had a yearning to teach at the college level and share my professional experiences and mentor others professionally, which is distinct from coaching. I had the academic credentials. I had the business experience and proven track record, but I did not have the tools to deliver an engaging classroom experience at the beginning of my new career path. The yearning was incredible and yet I knew I had to go to work and learn as much as I could if I was going to master the art and science of teaching. I attribute that yearning to carrying me through those difficult times, so I could obtain personal and professional mastery. I truly believe all things are possible with a yearning, effort, and persistence.

So, explore your possibilities. Explore your values. Explore your beliefs.

So, what do you yearn for in your life? Be specific and go for it!

Self-Assessment Questions

Question:
What do you yearn for?

Response:

Question:
Where do you start to make this happen?

Response:

Question:
What could stop you?

Response:

Question:
What is your timeline?

Response:

Question:

How will you measure success?

Response:

Coach/Mentor Questions

Q: What do you yearn for?

Response:

Q: Where do you start to make this happen?

Response:

Q: What could stop you?

Response:

Q: What is your timeline?

Response:

Q: How will you measure success?

Response:

Q: How can I support you?

Response:

Promotion Protocol

KIM NUGENT

ZONE

> "Everything is energy, and that's all there is to it. Match the frequency of the reality you want, and you can't help but get that reality. It can be no other way. This is not philosophy. This is physics.
> — Albert Einstein

Z IS FOR ZONE

I have often heard athletes describe being in the zone when everything they do seems to be going in the right direction. I am sure you have your favorite stories and examples, so you can imagine what being in the zone must feel like.

Being in the zone is described as being in the flow or flow state. Think back to a time when you lost track of time because you were in flow or the zone. Now that we have come to trait Z, number 26, do you feel you are in the zone? Have you ever been in the zone? What does it feel like? What were you doing? Describe the sensations.

If you are not in the zone now, how can you get back there? What is your energy level? What goals have you set? What actions are you taking? There is a great article written by Sarah Chang on "The Best Tricks for Getting in the Zone at Work." It can be retrieved at https://www.themuse.com/advice/the-best-tricks-for-getting-in-the-zone-at-work. She describes tools to get back into the flow state. What project can you be working on that challenges you? What goals do you want to accomplish? Can you create a space with little or few interruptions?

What are you not doing that you need to be doing? What should you keep doing that works? What should you stop doing? Are you committed to getting back to being in the zone state and take it to the next level? Turn off the TV and get started!

Self-Assessment Questions

Question:
Are you in the zone?

Response:

Question:
Describe when you were in the zone and how it felt.

Response:

Question:
Do you feel you are in the zone now?

Response:

Question:
How can you get back in the zone?

Response:

Question:

Read the article by Sarah Chang and check out the resources.

Response:

Question:

Final Reflection: Write out what you believe you have accomplished over the last 26 weeks. Be ready to discuss.

Response:

Question:

What is next?

Response:

Coach/Mentor Questions

Q: Are you in the zone?

Response:

Q: After reading the article by Sarah Chang what do you think?

Response:

Q: How can you help your team get in the zone?

Response:

Q: How can I support you?

Response:

Q: What have you learned?

Response:

Q: Final Reflection: Now that you have completed 26 weeks, what do you believe you have accomplished? Use the self-awareness inventory again to evaluate your progress.

Response:

Q: How have you changed?

Response:

Q: What is next?

Response:

Kim Nugent

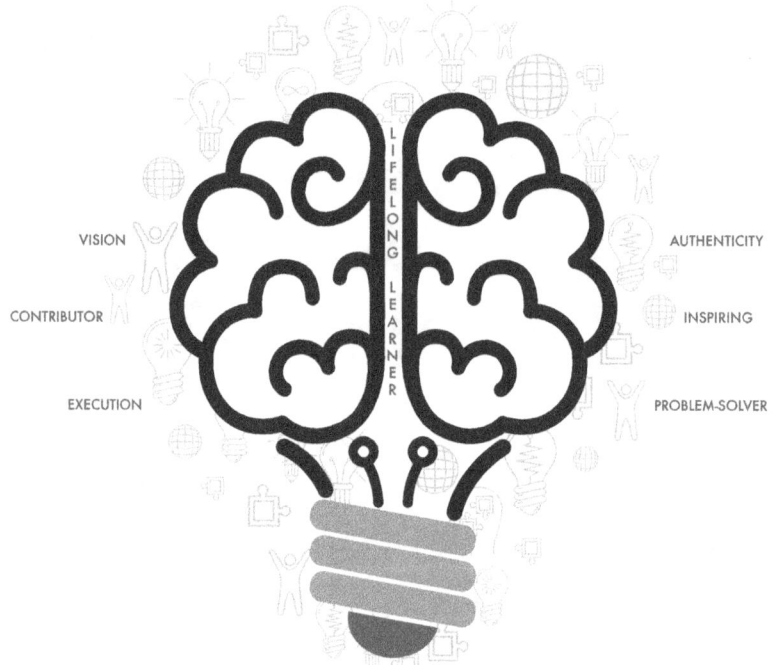

PROMOTION PROTOCOL™

www.PromotionProtocol.com

SELF-ASSESSMENT INVENTORY

Now that you have completed the 26 weeks, take the inventory again and explain how you have changed.

ABC's of Promotability	What have your learned? How have you changed in the last six months?
Rate Yourself 1-10. 1 Being Poor, 10 Being Excellent.	
1 2 3 4 5 6 7 8 9 10 Attitude	
1 2 3 4 5 6 7 8 9 10 Brand	
1 2 3 4 5 6 7 8 9 10 Communication	
1 2 3 4 5 6 7 8 9 10 Depth	
1 2 3 4 5 6 7 8 9 10 Energy	
1 2 3 4 5 6 7 8 9 10 Focus	
1 2 3 4 5 6 7 8 9 10 Gratitude	

ABC's of Promotability	What have your learned? How have you changed in the last six months?
Rate Yourself 1-10. 1 Being Poor, 10 Being Excellent.	
1 2 3 4 5 6 7 8 9 10 Habits	
1 2 3 4 5 6 7 8 9 10 Integrity	
1 2 3 4 5 6 7 8 9 10 Jaded	
1 2 3 4 5 6 7 8 9 10 Knowledgeable	
1 2 3 4 5 6 7 8 9 10 Life-Long Learner	
1 2 3 4 5 6 7 8 9 10 Mindset	
1 2 3 4 5 6 7 8 9 10 Network	
1 2 3 4 5 6 7 8 9 10 Opportunity	
1 2 3 4 5 6 7 8 9 10 Problem Solver	
1 2 3 4 5 6 7 8 9 10 Question	

ABC's of Promotability	What have your learned? How have you changed in the last six months?
Rate Yourself 1-10. 1 Being Poor, 10 Being Excellent.	
1 2 3 4 5 6 7 8 9 10 Responsibility	
1 2 3 4 5 6 7 8 9 10 Self-Awareness	
1 2 3 4 5 6 7 8 9 10 Thank You	
1 2 3 4 5 6 7 8 9 10 Unique	
1 2 3 4 5 6 7 8 9 10 Vision	
1 2 3 4 5 6 7 8 9 10 White Lies	
1 2 3 4 5 6 7 8 9 10 X-Factor	
1 2 3 4 5 6 7 8 9 10 Yearning	
1 2 3 4 5 6 7 8 9 10 Zone	

SUMMARY

This book is for you and about you. It is for your coach, supervisor, or mentor to use in your weekly coaching meetings. It is a guide to help you on your promotion pathway. It is a tool to become more self-aware. It is a framework to help bring you and your mentor closer to becoming better connected and sharing the same expectations. It will not happen overnight. After you complete twenty-six weeks of coaching and exercises, you should be very self-aware and able to demonstrate your engagement in the process. Now, you need to move into momentum on your pathway to promotability. I personally have had mentors and hired coaches throughout my career. The reason was to challenge my own thinking and achieve more powerful results in less time. I needed to get myself out of the way to look at alternative approaches and it worked every time. I want the same for you.

The reality of the workplace today has a dark side. You may have experienced this first hand, but you do not have to accept it. You can become an agent of change for making the workplace better. According to Randall Beck, Managing Partner, and Dr. Jim Harter,

Chief Scientist, at Gallup (2015), the state of the workplace is alarming and has not changed in the last twenty years (p. 1). The good news is that great managers create the right environment for engagement. The bad news, according to Beck and Harter, is that only 30% of U.S. employees are engaged and only 13% worldwide (p. 1). The solution is to acquire great talent and develop that talent.

Robert Hogan and Joyce Hogan, workplace assessment experts, (2001) stated between 50-75% of leaders are ineffective (p. 133). So, what explains the situation? In large part, these leaders have blind spots. They cannot connect, relate, hire well, coach, and develop people to build a team. They can be seen as micromanagers, negative and cynical. This results many times in an organizational failure. McKinsey and Company, global management consulting firm, (May, 2000) stated that only 10% of middle managers in the majority of firms qualify as real leaders and 30-50% of high-potential managers fail. So, given this alarming state of leadership ineffectiveness, what is the solution?

Just as we have described throughout this book, you need the combination of knowledge, skills, attitude, fit, and traits to be able to build high-performance teams. Could that be you?

Gallup also found that about one in ten people possess enough high talent to manage and another two in ten people exhibit some characteristics of managerial talent if the company invests in coaching and development (Beck & Harter, 2015, p. 2).

What is the root cause of the problem? It starts with making the right initial hire. This is where most companies miss the mark. Just because you have an opening do not rush to fill it. This will cost you. As I stated earlier, I create sayings that I live by. In this situation. I say to myself. "Desperation does not become you." The situation may feel desperate for you to fill the position but make sure you hire the best candidate, not just a warm body.

Once hired, you must coach and develop talent. Treat your employees the way you want to be treated. Didn't we learn that lesson in kindergarten? How come this lesson is so hard for some people?

The talent does exist in organizations; it just might not be the person in the current managerial or leadership role or one that has the title.

My personal career coaching track record is successful due in large part to finding the right candidates, then investing in each of them through weekly coaching sessions and facilitating leadership academies. Each time we had opportunities for promotion, I would think about all the employees in my organization one by one. What skills, traits, knowledge, and attitude did they possess? What were we looking for? Where would there be a good match? I have successfully used this approach for the past 20 years. I looked across the organization. I have never believed the career ladder is a straight line. I doubt you do, either. Assuming you are making the right hires, and holding weekly coaching meetings, you have to do more to develop your high-potential employees. We created a leadership academy to further develop these individuals in the organization. I am so proud of the hundreds of people I have coached and mentored to achieve the career of their dreams. I love celebrating their successes!

This culture has to be cultivated. The more you invest in your people, the higher returns in engagement, job satisfaction, productivity, and achieving performance indicators. If you just chase the metrics, your results will be short term.

There is another reality to the dark side of the workplace; the culture may not support you. If you have sought out a mentor or coach, completed all twenty-six activities, met weekly with your boss and nothing is changing, it might be time for you to consider another workplace. The truth is that sometimes employees get pigeon-holed or stuck for a variety of reasons. It could be mistakes the employee had made early on and everyone seems to remember. It could be the supervisor is personally threatened by developing employees. While hopefully these situations do not happen to you, you need to develop a succession plan to improve your future and get back on the pathway to promotability.

You have the tools to become a leader, which is distinct from being an exceptional leader. The reality is, there are very few exceptional leaders, but I am committed to changing your future, one conversation at a time.

If you want to learn more, check out *52 Weeks to Exceptional Leadership* by Dr. Kim Nugent to learn how to build that leadership muscle. If I can ever help you, please contact me at kim@drnugentspeaks.com as my passion is mentoring a new generation of exceptional leaders!

REFERENCES

Alton, L. (Sep. 7, 2016). *How sleep deprivation affects your day at the office.* Retrieved from https://www.forbes.com/sites/larryalton/2016/09/07/heres-how-sleep-affects-your-day-at-the-office/#3ed1c8e7820b

Anderson. L. & Krathwohl, D. (2001). *Revised Bloom's taxonomy.* Retrieved from https://thesecondprinciple.com/teaching-essentials/beyond-bloom-cognitive-taxonomy-revised/

Attitude. (2018). Retrieved from https://www.google.com/search?q=attitude+definition&oq=attitude+&aqs=chrome.5.69i57j35i39j0l4.5240j1j8&sourceid=chrome&ie=UTF-8

Beck, R. & Harter, J. (2015). *Managers account for 70% of the variance in employee engagement.* Retrieved from http://news.gallup.com/businessjournal/182792/managers-account-variance-employee-engagement.aspx

Bloom, B. (1956). *Bloom's taxonomy.* Retrieved from http://www.nwlink.com/~donclark/hrd/bloom.html

Brainy Quotes. (n.d.). Retrieved from https://www.brainyquote.com/

Bungay, G. (Jul 13, 2015). *Remarkable employees: The characteristics of high potentials.* Retrieved from http://performancecritical.com/remarkable-employees-characteristics-high-potentials/

Carnegie, D. (2013). *The five essential people skills: How to assert yourself, listen to others, and resolve conflicts.* Retrieved from https://www.youtube.com/watch?v=zvZbepIavY0

Cavoulous, A. (n.d.). *Ways to take on more responsibility at work.* Retrieved from https://www.themuse.com/advice/5-ways-to-take-on-more-responsibility-at-work

Chang, S. (n.d.). *The best tricks for getting in the zone at work.* Retrieved from https://www.themuse.com/advice/the-best-tricks-for-getting-in-the-zone-at-work.

Connellan, T. (2002). *Bringing out the best in others!: 3 keys for business leaders, educators, coaches, and parents.* Retrieved from https://www.amazon.com/Bringing-Out-Best-Others-Educators/dp/188516758X/ref=sr_1_1?ie=UTF8&qid=1520700987&sr=8-1&keywords=bringing+out+the+best+in+others

Dale Carnegie. (2018). Retrieved from https://www.dalecarnegie.com/en/franchise-locations

Dijulius, J. R. III (2003). *Secret service: Hidden systems that produce unforgettable customer service*. Retrieved from https://www.amazon.com/Secret-Service-Systems-Unforgettable-Customer/dp/0814471714/ref=sr_1_3?ie=UTF8&qid=1520797468&sr=8-3&keywords=secret+service+book

Dweck, C. (2009). *Mindset: How we can learn to fulfill our potential*. Retrieved from https://www.amazon.com/Mindset-Psychology-Carol-S-Dweck/dp/0345472322/ref=sr_1_1?ie=UTF8&qid=1518884922&sr=8-1&keywords=mindset+by+carol+dweck

Emmons, R. A. (2004). *The psychology of gratitude*. Retrieved from https://www.forbes.com/sites/larryalton/2016/09/07/heres-how-sleep-affects-your-day-at-the-office/#3ed1c8e7820b

Gordon, J. (2007). *How to deal with energy vampires*. Retrieved from http://www.jongordon.com/positive-tip-energy-vampires

Grammarly. (2018). Retrieved from https://www.grammarly.com

Hogan, R. & Hogan, J. (2001). Assessing leadership: a view of the dark side. *International Journal of Evaluation and Assessment*, 9, 40-51.

Holmes, L. (Dec. 2017). *10 things grateful people do differently.* Retrieved from https://www.huffingtonpost.com/entry/habits-of-grateful-people_us_565352a6e4b0d4093a588538

Kaiser, H. (n.d.). *What is problem-solving?* Retrieved from https://www.mindtools.com/pages/article/newTMC_00.htm

Liotta, A. (2012). *Unlocking generational codes: Understanding what makes the generations tick and what ticks them off.* Retrieved from http://resultance.com/

Maxwell, J. C. (2003). *Attitude 101: What every leader needs to know.* Retrieved from https://www.amazon.com/Attitude-101-Every-Leader-Needs/dp/0785263500

McKinsey and Co. (May, 2000). *Leadership development: Where is the ROI?* Retrieved from www.hri.eckerrd.edu

Moran, G. (2017). *Ditch these seven bad habits before 2018 starts.* Retrieved from https://www.fastcompany.com/40503547/ditch-these-seven-bad-habits-before-2018-starts

Myhre, M. (Nov. 2005). *Developing personal depth.* Retrieved from http://www.articlecity.com/articles/self_improvement_and_motivation/article_3237.shtml

National Speakers Association. (2018). Retrieved from https://www.nsaspeaker.org/

Peters, T. (2004). *Brand your survival kit.* Retrieved from https://www.fastcompany.com/48979/brand-you-survival-kit

Reynolds, J. (Mar 1, 2017). *20 characteristics of high-potential employees.* Retrieved from https://www.tinypulse.com/blog/20-characteristics-of-high-potential-employees

Rippy, R. (2017). *Love revolution: A 21-day program to create a life you love.* Retrieved from https://www.facebook.com/events/880164042160109/

Sinek, S. (2011). *Start with why: How great leaders inspire action.* Retrieved from https://www.ted.com/talks/simon_sinek_how_great_leaders_inspire_action

Ted Talks. (2018). Retrieved from https://www.youtube.com/channel/UCAuUUnT6oDeKwE6v1NGQxug

Toastmasters International (2018). Retrieved from https://www.toastmasters.org/

The Foundation for Critical Thinking. (2018). Retrieved from https://www.criticalthinking.org/

Yaffe, P. (Oct, 2011). *The 7% rule fact, fiction or misunderstanding.* doi: 10.1145/2043155.20453156.

ABOUT THE AUTHOR

Dr. Kim Nugent is an innovation leadership coach with an exceptional track record across generations of mentoring aspiring leaders into exceptional leadership positions. In addition, Kim is a best-selling author of the books: *Did I Say Never?* and *52 Weeks to Exceptional Leadership.*

Kim believes if you want to achieve extraordinary results, you must start with your people. Investing time, training, and mentoring to bring out the best in each individual is the first step in the process. The next step is to build a culture of sustainability through a customized mentoring system to achieve key performance indicators. If you would like to find out how, contact Kim at kim@promotionprotocol.com

www.ingramcontent.com/pod-product-compliance
Lightning Source LLC
Chambersburg PA
CBHW070129080526
44586CB00015B/1622